E   TS

Series Editor:
Bruce King

ENGLISH DRAMATISTS
Series Editor: Bruce King

Published Titles

Richard Cave, *Ben Jonson*
Christine Richardson and Jackie Johnston, *Medieval Drama*
Roger Sales, *Christopher Marlowe*

Forthcoming titles

Susan Bassnett, *Shakespeare: Elizabethan Plays*
Laura Bromley, *Webster and Ford*
John Bull, *Vanbrugh and Farquhar*
Philip McGuire, *Shakespeare: Jacobean Plays*
Kate McLuskie, *Dekker and Heywood*
Max Novak, *Fielding and Gay*
David Thomas, *William Congreve*
Cheryl Turner, *Early Women Dramatists*
Albert Wertheim, *Etherege and Wycherley*
Martin White, *Middleton and Tourneur*
Katharine Worth, *Sheridan and Goldsmith*

ENGLISH DRAMATISTS

CHRISTOPHER MARLOWE

Roger Sales

Lecturer in English Studies, University of East Anglia

MACMILLAN

First published 1991

Published by
MACMILLAN EDUCATION LTD
Houndmills, Basingstoke, Hampshire RG21 2XS
and London
Companies and representatives
throughout the world

Typeset by TecSet Ltd, Wallington, Surrey

Printed in Hong Kong

British Library Cataloguing in Publication Data
Sales, Roger
Christopher Marlowe. – (Macmillan English dramatists)
I. Title
822.3
ISBN 0–333–45351–4
ISBN 0–333–45352–2 pbk

In memory of Raymond Williams

Contents

Editor's Preface

Each generation needs to be introduced to the culture and great works of the past and to reinterpret them in its own ways. This series re-examines the important English dramatists of earlier centuries in the light of new information, new interests and new attitudes. The books are written for students, theatre-goers and general readers who want an up-to-date view of the plays and dramatists, with emphasis on drama as theatre and on stage, social and political history. Attention is given to what is known about performance, acting styles, changing interpretations, the stages and theatres of the time and theatre economics. The books will be relevant to those interested in or studying literature, theatre and cultural history.

BRUCE KING

Acknowledgements and Textual Notes

I am very grateful to Bruce King for asking me to write this book and for his sound advice during its various stages. I have also been helped by a group of Renaissance teachers at the University of East Anglia: David Aers, Sarah Beckwith (now at Duke University), Tony Gash, Vic Morgan and Peter Womack. I have benefited as well from discussions with a number of undergraduate and postgraduate students at East Anglia: Albert Chua, Gail Ching-Liang Low, Himansu Mohapatra, Jane Rondot and John Twyning. It is also a pleasure to acknowledge the institutional and intellectual support that I have received within my department while writing this book from Patricia Hollis and Roger Fowler. Anne, William and Jessica Sales have all helped in their own very special ways. The existence of the Royal Shakespeare Company's Swan Theatre has meant that there are now more opportunities to see Marlowe's plays in performance. It was fortunate that the period of my research and writing coincided with productions at Stratford of *The Jew of Malta*, *Doctor Faustus* and *Edward II*. The librarians at East Anglia and Cambridge have given me a lot of assistance, particularly those dealing with inter-library loans at East Anglia and rare books at Cambridge. I have dedicated this book to Raymond Williams in memory of the stimulating conversations we used to have about relationships between drama and dramatised societies.

Quotations from Marlowe's plays are taken from the 1971 Oxford University Press complete edition by Roma Gill, *The Plays of Christopher Marlowe*. The date in brackets after all plays cited refers to their first performance rather than to their publication. Many of these dates have to be based on guesswork. Spelling and punctuation have usually been modernised in the quotations from prose texts. References are given within the argument itself rather than in footnotes. Most prose quotations have been provided with a conventional page number. There are nevertheless a few occasions when Elizabethan pagination, a letter followed by a number, has had to be used. The following abbreviations have been used:

APC   John Roche Dasent (ed.), *Acts of the Privy Council of England* (1901, reprinted by Kraus Reprint, Nendeln/ Liechtenstein, 1974), volumes 14 and 24.

CH   Millar Maclure (ed.), *Marlowe: The Critical Heritage 1588–1896* (Routledge & Kegan Paul, London, 1979).

HC   Raphael Holinshed, *Holinshed's Chronicles of England, Scotland and Ireland* (1587, reprinted by AMS Press Inc., New York, 1965) 6 volumes.

ST   William Cobbett (ed.), *Cobbett's Complete Collection of State Trials and Proceedings for High Treason and other Crimes and Misdemeanors from the Earliest Period to the Present Day* (R. Bagshaw, London, 1809), 33 volumes, volume I.

Wernham R. B. Wernham, 'Christopher Marlowe at Flushing in 1592', *English Historical Review*, 91, 1976, pp.344–5.

The bibliography is divided into three sections. The first one identifies the texts that have been used and therefore fills in some of the gaps created by what I hope will be seen as the welcome absence of footnotes. The second section lists some of the secondary sources that have been used in the reconstruction of Elizabethan society. It also includes books and articles on Marlowe which are primarily of biographical rather than critical importance. Many students might wish to go straight to the third section, which lists some of the books and articles on Marlowe's plays and the

Elizabethan theatre. Those that have been starred are the ones that I consider to be particularly useful.

This short study concentrates on the five plays by Marlowe that are most frequently studied and performed. It includes references to *The Tragedy of Dido, Queen of Carthage* and *The Massacre at Paris*, although they are not dealt with at length. The Bibliography nevertheless includes material on all of Marlowe's plays.

Part One:

The Dramatised Society

1
The Educational Stage

1.1 The Theatre of Politics

Sir Walter Ralegh wrote *The History of the World* (1614) during his long imprisonment in the Tower of London. He was confined there on 16 December 1603 after being tried at Winchester for high treason. London was not felt to be the appropriate location for the trial because of the heat of the plague. Although he was found guilty of conspiring with Spain, his sentence was commuted to imprisonment at almost the last moment. He remained a prisoner until he was publicly executed on 29 October 1618. The only break in this regime came in 1616, when he was released to lead a second expedition to Guiana to try to discover gold. It can be argued, however, that he also released himself from close confinement by writing *The History of the World*. The grand gesture of attempting to record world history became a way of transcending physical restrictions, at the same time as drawing attention to them. King James I decreed a little room, but he could not stop Ralegh using it for great reckonings.

Ralegh proved at his trial that he was still a great actor. His imprisonment therefore deprived an actor of his audience. World history became a stage on which the imprisoned actor could still perform both for himself and for his readers. The seemingly obscure subject of Assyrian history provides him with one of his many cues to make a deceptively casual entrance:

... I remember a pretty jest of *Don Pedro de Sarmiento*, a worthy Spanish Gentleman, who had been employed by his King in planting a Colony upon the straits of *Magellan*; for when I asked him, being then my Prisoner, some question about an Island in those straits, which me thought, might have done either benefit or displeasure to his enterprise, he told me merrily, that it was to be called the *Painter's Wife's Island*; saying, that whilst the fellow drew that Map, his wife sitting by, desired him to put in one Country for her; that she, in imagination, might have an Island of her own. (Bk.2, Ch.23, Pt. 4, p. 574)

He casts himself as an explorer and man of action who is devoted to the service of his country. He may be a prisoner now and yet he once held prisoners himself. The Spanish are the enemy although he, as befits a true leader, is still able to treat them humanely and courteously. The desire of the mapmaker's wife for immortality becomes a comic debasement of the way in which he himself named Virginia after Queen Elizabeth. The mapmaker's wife only has an island 'in imagination'. Ralegh was nevertheless able to combine imagination with action. The casually delivered anecdote allows the actor to stage a version of himself and his enemies.

Stephen Greenblatt argues in *Sir Walter Ralegh: The Renaissance Man and His Roles* (1973) that *The History of the World* is profoundly contradictory. At one level, Ralegh's belief in the existence of stage-play worlds leads to a fatalistic resignation to the will of God. The human tragedy is a divinely-authored play in which there is no escape from the part as written, even though the nature of the part might well remain obscure until the very end of the play. This orthodox view lies behind the presentation of Bajazeth, who is appointed by God to act the part of the Turkish Emperor, but does not know that he has also been cast to play the part of Tamburlaine's footstool. At another level, however, Greenblatt argues that Ralegh is obsessed by the way in which political stages offer himself and others opportunities to mould and fashion themselves. Although he was barely a gentleman by birth, his own imagination and actions necessitated the re-drawing of the map of the world.

Greenblatt explores the theme of self-fashioning in Ralegh's other writings suggesting, for instance, some of the ways in which his poetry allows him to act out an elaborate courtship ritual with Queen Elizabeth. These written texts are complemented by the way in which Ralegh played the part of the courtier through the ways in which he fashioned and displayed his own body. The poet himself, dressed in silver armour and dripping with jewels, was an exquisite dramatic text. The treason trial, the expeditions to Guiana and the execution are taken by Greenblatt to be plays in which Ralegh cast himself as the main character. He did not, for instance, deliver his speech from the scaffold until he had made sure that the spectators were in the correct positions. His performances in both Ireland and Parliament need to be added to Greenblatt's list of dramatic texts.

The first part of this study of Marlowe offers a reconstruction of the dramatised nature of Elizabethan society. It will not concentrate on colonial expeditions, although trials, plague epidemics, prisons and public executions will figure prominently. Prose writings will be seen as providing stages for their writers. The body and its costumes will be read as dramatic texts. Forms of educational and street theatre will also be considered in an attempt to identify the various stages that existed beyond the theatres themselves. The events of Marlowe's life will be outlined, although the aim is to recover some of the distinctive features of the Elizabethan mentality rather than to be confined to the personal history of an important writer. This means that the world of the spectator will be considered as well as that of the author. One way of thinking about the relationship between the two parts of this study is to see the work on the dramatised society as providing contexts for the drama itself. A better way of describing the relationship is to see both parts as offering readings of a range of Elizabethan dramatic texts with a view to identifying how spectators might have responded to them.

1.2 Two Cambridge Disputes

Marlowe was born and brought up in Canterbury, the religious capital of England. He was christened on 26 February 1564. His father, John Marlowe, was a moderately prosperous tradesman who was a member of the shoemakers' guild and a freeman of the city. He also seems to have been immoderately quarrelsome, even by Elizabethan standards. His will, together with that of his wife, indicates financial security rather than prosperity.

Marlowe entered the King's School at Canterbury on a scholarship in 1579. The curriculum, in common with other Elizabethan secondary schools, was based on the study of Latin grammar, together with Roman history and literature. Scholars were also expected to sing in the cathedral choir. This schooling prepared Marlowe for entrance to Corpus Christi College, Cambridge. He was, once again, awarded a scholarship to continue his studies. Matthew Parker, the first Elizabethan Archbishop of Canterbury, was one of the college's main benefactors. He established a number of scholarships both during his lifetime and through the terms of his will in 1575. He also bequeathed his library to the college. Marlowe entered Corpus in December 1580 on one of Parker's scholarships. He was formally admitted, or matriculated, in March 1581 at the age of seventeen. He would have been older than many of his contemporaries since it was customary for Elizabethan students to attend university at an earlier age than is common today. The university statutes stipulated fourteen as the minimum age for a scholar. Students from aristocracy and gentry, who were not dependent on scholarships, could and often did begin their university careers even earlier. Scholarships allowed Marlowe to become a member of an elite society from which he would otherwise have been excluded. Those who read his plays autobiographically often notice that they contain socially marginalised characters who are determined to assert their centrality.

Marlowe shared a converted 'storehouse' with three other Parker scholars. Such conversions provide an indication of the expansion of the university during the sixteenth century, which was partly as a result of its increasing importance for aristocratic education. Marlowe's scholarship was initially to allow him to prepare for a bachelor of arts degree, with the possibility of an extension to enable him to proceed to a master of arts degree. He took his BA in 1584. The curriculum was largely based around the study of grammar, rhetoric and dialectic, which was known as the Trivium. Examinations were oral rather than written ones. A student was expected either to defend or attack a particular proposition in a 'dialectic' with his contemporaries. This verbal combat, or bout, took place in front of an audience and was moderated by more senior members of the university. Credit was given for facility and fluency, as well as for the selection and arrangement of material. The dialectical method provided a platform, or stage, for the articulation of unorthodox or even monstrous opinions to challenge traditional positions.

The performance of a certain Mr Boyes in the Old Schools at Cambridge towards the end of the Elizabethan era is described by William T. Costello in *The Scholastic Curriculum at Early Seventeenth-Century Cambridge* (1958) (pp. 19–24). Boyes elected to defend the thesis that the threat of punishment provided a deterrent from crime. This was, in theory, an orthodox position which was re-affirmed each and every time a spectacle of suffering was staged on the scaffold to remind the spectators of their duties and allegiances. The fact that the spectacle had to be staged so regularly casts considerable doubt on the theory. Boyes was introduced to both the other actors and the spectators by his 'father', who was a senior member of his college. Academic father and son processed to this theatre of education in company with other members of the college. They performed in front of an audience which consisted of other examinees, more junior students there for the experience and other members of the university. Boyes started off by spending half an hour making a prepared defence of his thesis. This play had a script although, as will be seen, it also included improvisations. Boyes's 'father' then commented on his performance and also raised a few minor objections to the argument. This set the scene for the main theatrical event. Boyes's first opponent offered a critique of the thesis and then a second opponent tried to trap him through a series of syllogistic questions. This second opponent was so confident of victory that at one point he declared that 'I will slit your throat with your own sword'. Boyes nevertheless tenaciously stuck to his thesis and prevented his own arguments from being turned against him. There is, unfortunately, no record of what was said by the moderator, or examiner, at the conclusion of this particular dispute. It can probably be assumed that the spectators were allowed to be more active during the more improvised parts of the play. College rivalries might have led to a mixed, and often noisy, reception on this particular occasion. The actors probably employed a range of highly theatrical gestures. François Rabelais offers a satire in *Pantagruel* (1532) on the complex sign language that was employed in disputations. Panurge combats it with his own particular brand of grotesque gestures. It is clear that the more prestigious public disputes in Cambridge also provided opportunities for carnivalesque performances by a prevaricator.

Boyes defended an orthodox Elizabethan position and so his opponents were encouraged to produce dissenting arguments. It would still be dangerous to take a utopian view of the dialectic, or dialogic, structure of Elizabethan society. As will become apparent, Queen Elizabeth and her ministers staged public punishments and other displays of power in order to discourage what was known as diversity in opinions. Yet they could not always control how such spectacles were received. The real weakness in Boyes's argument is that it does not question assumptions about uniform reception. A spectacle that was staged to promote uniformity might well provoke the very diversity in opinions that it should have been policing.

Marlowe was awarded his BA degree and decided to stay on to prepare for his MA. This probably meant having to give some general assurances to his college that he intended to enter the Church. This is not to say that the three year MA programme was devoted to any great extent to theological studies. The emphasis was in fact on classical philosophy, which embraced related subjects such as astronomy. Yet, in the case of a Parker scholar, it was probably clearly understood that such further study was a general means to quite a specific end. It is impossible to say whether Marlowe's decision to remain at Cambridge represented a self-conscious stratagem by which, under the colour of training for the Church, he bought the time to begin his literary career. All that can be said is that it was during these last years at Cambridge that this literary career began to take shape. He produced translations of classical poetry. He also wrote *Dido, Queen of Carthage*, which may have been first performed in Norwich and Ipswich during the earlier part of 1587. Corpus, through Archbishop Parker's connections, had strong ties with East Anglia. The play was performed later by 'the children of Her Majesties Chappell'. Marlowe probably produced most, if not all, of the first part of *Tamburlaine the Great* before leaving Cambridge in 1587. The instant popularity of this play when it was first performed in London in the same year encouraged him to write a sequel.

It was not just a literary career that was forged in these final years in the 'storehouse'. An entry in the *Acts of the Privy Council* on 29 June 1587 refers to a dispute between Marlowe and the university authorities over whether he should be allowed to proceed to the MA degree. The document conceals as much as it reveals. The college accounts show that Marlowe's attendance became erratic during his last years. He was, for instance, absent for several months during the earlier part of 1587. Elizabethan students were expected to remain in almost permanent residence. More specifically, the terms of Marlowe's scholarship permitted him only a month's vacation every year. It seems probable that rumours began to circulate around Cambridge as to why he was failing to fulfil his residence requirements. A likely explanation, given the religious climate of the 1580s, was that he had gone abroad to convert to Catholicism. John Ballard, a student at Gonville and Caius College, disappeared to the seminary in Rheims in 1579. He returned to England and, as will be seen, was eventually publicly executed along with the other Babington conspirators in 1586. The Privy Council document makes it reasonably clear that the university authorities had formed the opinion that Marlowe, or Morley as he is referred to here, was also part of a Catholic network:

> Whereas it was reported that Christopher Morley was deter-mined to have gone beyond the seas to Rheims and there to remain, their Lordships thought good to certify that he had no such intent but that in all his actions he had behaved himself orderly and discreetly, whereby he had done her Majesty good service, and deserved to be rewarded for his faithful dealing; their Lordships' request was that the rumour thereof should be allayed by all possible means, and that he should be furthered in the degree he was to take this next Commencement; because it was not her Majesty's pleasure that any one employed as he had been in matters touching the benefit of his country should be defamed by those that are ignorant in the affairs he went about. (APC, 15, p. 141)

This sharp reprimand from the Privy Council ensured that the twenty-three year old student won his dispute with the university authorities.

Marlowe had become a member of the secret service during his last years at Cambridge. Some of his absences from college may have coincided with relatively low-grade employment as a messenger. It is possible that he was actually planted at Rheims and yet the Privy Council document tries to clear his name by focussing attention on the specific charge that he intended, or 'determined', to go there. It therefore seems more likely that his job was to provide information about potential converts in Cambridge itself. Anyone with the genuine intention of going to Rheims would not want such information to become public knowledge. Marlowe, by contrast, had to be a little more open about his feigned intentions otherwise he might not have been able to come into contact with his prey. Such a technique, or practice, was standard procedure in the secret service. As will become more apparent, government spies gave out that they were regicides or just Catholic supporters in order to bait a trap for the unwary.

2
The Theatre of Hell

2.1 Enter Poley

The Elizabethan intelligence service was masterminded by Sir
Francis Walsingham. He learnt at least some of his tradecraft
while he was Ambassador to France from 1570 to 1573. Embassies
played an important part in the gathering of intelligence. When
Walsingham returned to England to take up the powerful position
of Secretary, he made sure that he was informed about the comers
and goers at various embassies in both London and continental
Europe. This involved having buildings watched from the outside,
as well as either recruiting or placing informers inside. It also
involved intercepting correspondence. Walsingham's agents kept
the ports as well as the embassies under close surveillance. The
intelligence that was gathered in these ways was brought to him
either by the agents themselves, or else by professional mes-
sengers. It usually arrived in code. The ciphers that have survived
are based upon one set of symbols for the letters of the alphabet
and another set for names, places and technical terms. They
usually contained some irrelevant symbols designed to make the
code harder to crack. Walsingham did not receive a grant for these
activities until the beginning of the 1580s and so probably had to
finance some of his earlier operations out of his own pocket.

   Plenty of information nevertheless came through what can be
described as open sources. Somebody with a particular piece of

gossip might communicate it openly to Walsingham. Perhaps the university authorities did just this when they picked up rumours that Marlowe was intending to defect to Rheims. The precarious nature of the European balance of power also called for less straightforward practices. The intelligence service relied upon two types of agent. First of all, it utilised the services of members of the gentry, particularly if they happened to be living abroad. Anthony Bacon, the elder brother of Francis Bacon, built up his own European intelligence network during the 1580s and put it at the disposal of both Walsingham and William Cecil, Lord Burghley. He became an expert on French politics. He was expected to finance the operation himself and let others take the credit for it. He switched his loyalties to the Earl of Essex in the 1590s. Walsingham also used his cousin, Thomas Walsingham, as an agent throughout the 1580s. Thomas Walsingham became Marlowe's literary patron. The English Agent who appears at the end of Marlowe's *The Massacre at Paris* (1593) has access to the French court and may be a representation of a gentry agent.

Marlowe himself belongs to the second category of agent, namely educated young men who fetched their gentry from the universities rather than from heraldry. Thomas Rogers, alias Berden, began his career by supplying information about the activities of Catholic priests in England, but was then gradually able to insinuate himself into influential positions within the Catholic community. He was therefore able to supply inside information. The evidence suggests that he developed his own form of insider trading: accepting bribes from suspects on the understanding that he would put in a good word for them. It was not money well spent since his recommendations did not carry much weight. Robert Poley was another educated young man who made a career in the secret service. He appears to have started as an informer in the Marshalsea Prison. Just as Marlowe let it be known in Cambridge that he intended to go to the seminary at Rheims, so Poley attempted to gain the confidences of Catholic prisoners by giving out that he supported their cause. The Marshalsea acquired a reputation for the relative freedom enjoyed by its political prisoners. The Bishop of London declared that it was just like a seminary because Catholics were able to practise their religion openly and so entice others to join them. It is possible that Poley attempted to get close to Ben Jonson when he was in the Marshalsea in 1597 for writing topical satire.

It would be misleading to imply that Walsingham's secret service was particularly sophisticated. He received no money until the 1580s. Lessons also had to be learnt through trial and error. Francis Throgmorton was arrested in 1583 as a result of routine surveillance on the French Embassy in London. He revealed on the rack the existence of plans for an invasion by the Duke of Guise. It might have been better, however, to have kept him under surveillance for longer so all of his accomplices could have been traced.

2.2 Street Theatre

Walsingham had obviously learnt from the mistake of Throgmorton's hasty arrest by the time he came to play his endgame with the Babington conspirators in 1586. This time he was much better informed about the activities of the Catholics both at home and abroad. This was partly because he had persuaded Gilbert Gifford, a prominent member of the seminary at Rheims, to play the part of a double-agent. He was therefore able to anticipate the stealthy movements of priests like Ballard when they returned to England. He did not, however, have to rely solely on Gifford's information. One of his agents, Bernard Maude, became Ballard's servant. Maude had been imprisoned in the Fleet for blackmailing the Archbishop of York over a sexual relationship. It may be that Maude came to Walsingham's notice by supplying information on Catholic prisoners in the Fleet. He was certainly released early and insinuated himself into the Catholic community.

Some historians claim that the secret service, through its informers and *agents provocateurs*, staged the Babington conspiracy as the necessary dramatic prologue for the execution of Mary, Queen of Scots, at the beginning of 1587. This may be overstating the case, although it is certainly true that Walsingham was able to cue most of the entrances and exits in this political drama. He decided to make it easier for Catholics to communicate with the Queen of Scots in the hope that letters would eventually incriminate both them and her. Gifford, who was trusted by Mary and her advisers, was employed to establish a supposedly secret postal service which could nevertheless be tapped into by Walsingham. Messages were smuggled in and out of Chartley, where Mary was being kept under close house arrest, in beer barrels. Mary and her supporters were unaware that the brewer, who acted as their courier, was also on Walsingham's payroll. He was, ironically, given the codename of 'the honest man'.

One of the results of allowing Mary to send and receive letters was to put her in contact with a group of young Catholic gentlemen, a number of whom were associated with the Inns of Court. They were happy enough to cast themselves as conspirators in the taverns of Chancery Lane and Fleet Street. They discussed plans to rescue Mary over meals and drinks in the Castle, the Three Tuns and the Plough. Chidiock Titchbourne claimed, as he stood on the scaffold waiting to be executed, that everybody in the streets knew that he and his special male friend were the real roaring boys:

> Of whom went report in the Strand, Fleet Street and elsewhere about London but of Babington and Titchbourne? No threshold was of force to brave our entry. (ST, p. 1157)

Careless tavern talk could cost lives since it was high treason even to imagine the death of Queen Elizabeth. Charles Tilney was not one of Anthony Babington's intimate friends, but was present one evening at the Three Tuns when the roaring boys were arguing about the best way of killing the Queen. He made the eminently practical, if somewhat guarded, suggestion that 'it might be her majesty might be set upon in her coach' (ST, p. 1150). He himself was set upon by the executioner for letting his imagination run riot.

Babington fashioned himself into a charismatic figure in the streets and student bars. Did he dream of marrying Mary, Queen of Scots, and riding in triumph with her through London? It would have been passing brave. He was nevertheless dragged in disgrace through the streets on a hurdle because he remained unaware almost until the end that Walsingham had decided to fashion him into a grotesque traitor. Enter Poley, playing a loyal Catholic who admired a man of action like Babington who could force his way across any threshold. Such flattery only worked for a brief time and then Babington started to suffer from stage fright. He decided to go abroad. Enter Poley once more, this time offering to use connections which did not point to any involvement in the secret service, to arrange for Babington to have an interview with Walsingham in order to get a licence to travel abroad. Babington met Walsingham and volunteered to undertake intelligence work for him abroad, if the licence was forthcoming. He offered to spy for the very man who was spying upon him. Walsingham kept his options open. It seems reasonably clear that, by this stage in the theatrical game, Walsingham and Poley were acting at cross purposes. Poley appears to have been working on the assumption that Babington had been cast to play the part of an informer, who was meant to send his fellow conspirators to the scaffold. Walsingham, by contrast, wanted Babington himself to play the part of a traitor. Some of this confusion is indicated by Walsingham's guarded note about Poley, which is quoted in Alan Gordon Smith's *The Babington Plot* (1936): 'though I do not find but that Poley hath dealt honestly with me, yet I am loath to lay myself any way open unto him' (p. 184). Poley may have been ignorant of how the dramatist had written the final act and yet he still had important functions to fulfil. The irony of Babington offering to be a spy is capped by the way in which he ended up staying at Poley's house because he was convinced that his own lodgings were being watched.

Ballard was the first to be arrested. He had begun to consider the possibility that the government might know more about the conspiracy than the conspirators themselves did. He did not, however, suspect the open and accommodating Poley, although by this stage it was clear to him that Maude was in fact one of Walsingham's good angels. Ballard wrote to Walsingham with an offer of information about the conspiracy. It was declined because he, too, had been cast to play the part of a grotesque traitor. There was some justification for this casting since he had been involved in discussions of regicide with leading European and English Catholics. He also supplied the regulars at the Three Tuns with timely reminders about their promises when their thirst for action, rather than acting, was in danger of being too easily quenched.

Priests had to disguise their true identities to prevent themselves being thrown into prison and befriended by Walsingham's spies. One of Ballard's best characters, or aliases, was Captain

Fortescue, a dashing soldier who was on his way to join the Earl of Leicester's army in the Low Countries. One of his entrances as this character was described during Tilney's trial:

> being a popish priest, he came in a grey cloak laid on with gold lace, in velvet hose, a cut satin doublet, a fair hat of the newest fashion, the band being set with silver buttons; a man and boy after him, and his name Captain Fortescue. (ST, p. 1150)

Ballard may have tried to strengthen the resolve of the conspirators and yet this account of his activities suggests that he shared their delight in self-fashioning. The man who dogged his footsteps disguised as a servant was Maude, the blackmailer of the Archbishop of York, who was now employed to protect the Church and State. The boy may have been the only person present who was playing himself.

Other priests assumed similar disguises. John Gerard lived and dressed like a courtier. He avoided suspicion on one occasion by allowing himself to be seen gambling at cards. A touring theatrical company known as Cholmely's Men was investigated by the Star Chamber in 1610. It was suspected of allowing priests to disguise themselves as actors so that they could be smuggled between the homes of the Catholic gentry in Yorkshire. Actors certainly played priests in plays by Marlowe and others, so perhaps priests were acting the parts of actors.

Captain Fortescue was by no means the only counterfeit soldier who paraded the streets of London. Those who patched themselves up to look like wounded soldiers could expect some assistance from the State in the form of licences to travel and to beg. Shakespeare's Ancient Pistol proves that he knows how to play this part. The Privy Council was well aware that it was being played. It wrote to the Lord Mayor of London in November 1586 to demand that beggars and vagabonds who counterfeited wounded soldiers should be severely punished. One of the problems involved in implementing this policy was that the distinction between the vagabond and the soldier was often not a very clear one. Vagabonds and other members of the criminal underworld were frequently pressed into military service. The muster lists were not as helpful as they might have been in distinguishing between the true and the counterfeit soldier. It was common practice for the lists to include either purely fictitious names, or else those of dead soldiers, so that the officers could make their profit. Counterfeit soldiers marched around the stages as well as the streets of Elizabethan London in plays by Jonson, Thomas Dekker and others.

Walsingham allowed the Babington conspirators enough rope to hang themselves. He was even considerate enough to provide them with most of the rope. His waiting game eventually produced an incriminating exchange of letters between Mary, Queen of Scots, and her gallant admirers. Babington's letter declared that 'All the actors have vowed, either to die, or else to perform their purpose . . .' (ST, p. 1146). Walsingham was nevertheless reluctant to appear on stage to acknowledge the applause. He deliberately left his own name off the warrants that were drawn up for the arrest of the conspirators because he did not want to be seen in the matter. Poley was able to make sure that Ballard, alias Captain Fortescue, was apprehended with no difficulty. The other conspirators were allowed to escape and it took over a week for them to be caught. Babington and some others hid out in St John's Wood. They cut their hair short and stained their faces with walnut-juice. William Camden's *Annales: The True and Royal History of the Famous Empress Elizabeth Queen of England* (1625) records that they also tried to disguise themselves by wearing 'rustic apparell' (Bk. 3, p. 139). The sumptuary legislation on apparel was designed to make sure that costume corresponded to social identity. It was constantly being flouted not just by priests and counterfeit soldiers, but also by those who quite literally dressed up their social status. The young gentlemen who took part in the Babington conspiracy reversed this trend by dressing down.

The attempts that were made to capture the conspirators produced moments of farce amidst the high political drama. Burghley, the most influential man in the land, was returning to London by coach on 10 August 1586. He had attacked Catholic priests as being stirrers of sedition in *The Execution of Justice in England* (1583):

Let it be answered why they came thus by stealth into the realm. Why they have wandered up and down in corners in disguised sort, changing their titles, names, and manner of apparel. (p. 37)

He noticed groups of men standing around by the roadside and at first thought that they were just sheltering from rain under overhanging roofs. It was only when he got to Enfield, where it was not raining, that he realised that these groups consisted of the watchmen who were supposed to apprehend the missing conspirators. He stopped the coach and

> asked them whereto they stood there and one of them answered, to take 3 young men: and demanding how they should know the persons, one answered with these words "Marry my Lord, by intelligence of their favour". "What mean you by that", quod I: "Marry", said they "one of the parties hath a hooked nose" "And have you" quoth I, "no other mark?" "No" sayeth they. (As quoted in *Reliquary*, April 1862, p. 174)

Burghley was not amused by his encounter with the watchmen of Enfield. He told Walsingham that badly instructed watchmen, who displayed themselves so openly, had little chance of apprehending stealthy rogues. The watchmen appear to have been waiting to arrest Jewish rather than Catholic conspirators.

2.3 Outward Show

The eventual arrest of the conspirators was greeted with jubilation in London and also, perhaps, in Enfield. Camden records that the loyal citizens rang bells, lit bonfires and sang psalms. Elizabeth wrote from Windsor on 18 August 1586 to thank the Lord Mayor for these celebrations. She states in *The True Copy of a Letter from the Queenes Majesty to the Lord Mayor and his Brethren* (1586)

> that we did not so much rejoice at the escape of the intended attempt against our own person, as to see the great joy our most loving subjects took at the apprehension of the contrivers thereof, which, to make their love more apparent they have (as we are to our great comfort informed) omitted no outward show, that by any external act might witness to the

world the inward love and dutiful affection they bear towards
us. (A2)

Elizabethans defined themselves and their society through a whole
series of outward shows. This letter, for example, was not just part
of a personal correspondence between the Queen and the Lord
Mayor but was also, as the full title goes on to note, 'read openly in
a great assembley of the Commons in the Guildhall of that city, the
22 day of August 1586'. It was, of course, also published.
Elizabeth suggests that an 'outward show' provided a necessary
manifestation, but also an elaboration, of more private feelings.
Her version does not acknowledge an instability in the relationship
between the 'external' and the 'inward'. The history of the
Babington conspiracy nevertheless indicates that confusion over
the meanings of shows and signs was a distinctive feature of the
stage-play world. It also illustrates the ways in which such confu-
sions were acknowledged through the way in which they were
exploited both by the government and its enemies. Elizabeth's
own 'outward show' of relief at the discovery of the conspiracy did
not bear witness to the fact that she had been kept informed about
the activities in and around the Three Tuns from a relatively early
stage. She also knew all about the deceits being practised by 'the
honest man'.

The main charge against the conspirators, as Elizabeth's letter
indicates, was that they had tried to commit regicide. Their
schemes to release Mary, Queen of Scots, and to prepare the way
for a foreign invasion were technically of secondary importance.
John Savage, encouraged by Gilbert Gifford and others, had taken
an oath in Rheims to assassinate Elizabeth. He was assured that,
because she had been excommunicated by the Pope in 1570, he
would not be committing a sin. He found, however, that acting out
an elaborate initiation ritual and carrying out the action itself were
two very different things. He therefore invented a whole series of
excuses for postponing the hour of Elizabeth's death. His Mephostophilis, in the shapes of Gifford, Ballard and Babington,
periodically reminded him about his contract. Yet how, he pro-
tested, could he even get near Elizabeth when he did not have the
right clothes to make an appearance at court? He thought that it
was absolutely essential for him to be able to disguise his inward

intentions with the outward show of a loyal courtier. The assassination was eventually planned, or imagined, to be undertaken by six men.

Regicide obviously involved the ultimate violation of Elizabeth's natural body. It was also an assault on her other, or ceremonial, body. This second body incarnated the spiritual essence of monarchy and was technically immune from destruction. This meant, nevertheless, that the regicide struck a blow against the country's past and future as well as against its present. The blow could never ultimately succeed but even to imagine it, let alone execute or compass it, was high treason. The Elizabethans had particularly vivid imaginations. Edward Squire dreamt up the idea of poisoning the Queen's saddle in 1597. Like Tilney, he believed that Elizabeth was at her most vulnerable when she was travelling. Her movement around London and the rest of the kingdom displayed her power and yet it was also when she was potentially at her weakest.

The assassination of the Protestant Prince of Orange in 1584 was regarded by many Elizabethans as being too close to home for comfort. The assassin had to endure an exceptionally long period of public torture before his eventual execution. Anxieties about regicide led to the recruitment of Dr William Parry, who was briefed to approach Catholics with proposals to murder Elizabeth in the hope of identifying a true regicide. It seems that he acted too much on his own initiative as he himself was publicly executed on 2 March 1585 for imagining the Queen's death. He attracted hostility from the spectators at both his trial and execution because he refused to stick to his original confession of guilt. He may have made unauthorised approaches to Catholics in the hope of being able to blackmail them over indiscreet remarks. Most agents engaged in freelance activities. Poley accepted fifty pounds from Babington as a fee for providing the introduction to Walsingham, while he was also putting Walsingham's money in his purse for keeping Babington under surveillance. Babington also gave him a diamond as a token, or outward show, of their friendship.

Walsingham may not have liked appearing on the stage itself and yet he was very busy behind the scenes after the arrest of the Babington conspirators. His main activity was to prepare the script for the trials by making sure that it included signed confessions of guilt. The existence of such documents meant that the trials were not designed to debate the evidence but, rather, to provide a theatrical display to satisfy the people that the Queen's death had been imagined. Savage was the first to be tried because his oath to kill Elizabeth, which was held to be a demonic inversion of social and religious rituals, represented the real threat. Although the conspiracy became associated with Babington's name, Walsingham regarded Savage and Ballard as his main targets. Babington himself played an undistinguished part in the courtroom at Westminster Hall, endeavouring to lay all the blame upon Ballard. Sir Christopher Hatton was nevertheless prepared to accept at least a version of Babington's account. He was primarily concerned to break down Ballard's outward show so that the inward activities of Catholic priests could be displayed for all to see:

> Nay, Ballard, you must say more and shall say more, for you must not commit High-Treasons and then huddle them up; but is this thy *Religio Catholica*? Nay rather, it is *Diabolica*. (ST, p. 1138)

Misrule is imagined by alien strangers and can only be described in a foreign tongue. Hatton used Ballard's activities not only to justify existing legislation against Catholics, but also to press for harsher penalties in the future:

> The inventers and beginners whereof were these devilish priests and seminaries, against whom he doubted the parliament had not yet sufficiently provided . . . (ST, p. 1140)

The good angels made the most of their capture of the bad angels.
The leading conspirators were tried on 13 and 14 September 1586. Savage emphatically denied that torture had been used to extract a confession from him. The fullness of Babington's confession suggests that Walsingham might have adopted a more subtle approach: putting on an outward show to suggest that cooperation might lead to a commuted sentence at the same time as he was preparing to demand the most severe penalties. The remaining conspirators were tried on 15 September, although the verdicts were a foregone conclusion given the events of the previous two days. Some of the accused, such as John Travers, saw the writing on the wall and entered half-hearted defences. Others like Robert

Gage took the opportunity to flout the solemnity of the proceedings. When he was asked why he had fled to the woods with some of the other conspirators, he 'stoutly and fiercely answered, For company' (ST, p. 1154). Tilney and Edward Abington did their best to resist charges which were based on little more than guilt by association. They both tried unsuccessfully to raise points of legal interpretation with the prosecution. Although the Elizabethan laws on treason required that it had to be proved by two witnesses who were not themselves on trial, earlier legislation was not so particular. When Abington asked for such witnesses to be produced, he was told that he was being tried under this earlier legislation. He was also unsuccessful when he requested tables for his papers:

> Then said Abington, I beseech your honours I may have a pair of writing-tables to set down what is alledged against me, that I may yield a sufficient Answer thereunto.
> *Sandes*   It was never the course here.
> *Hatton*   When you hear any thing you are desirous to answer, you shall speak an Answer at full, which is better than a pair of tables. (ST, p. 1143)

Sandes was the Clerk of the Court. Abington wished to colonise a part of this particular political stage with props which could be identified as belonging to him. Although Ralegh managed to do this at his trial in 1603, Abington's request was rejected because it would have led to some disruption of the outward show of power. Territorial rights were being asserted not just as far as the courtroom itself was concerned, but also in relation to the streets around the Inns of Court. The students were allowed to elect a carnival prince as part of their Christmas revels. He held court and was licensed to lead a mock procession through the city to the Tower of London. It was, however, high treason to imagine forms of unauthorised carnival and misrule.

2.4 The Theatre of Hell

John Stubbes was publicly punished for writing against Queen Elizabeth's proposed marriage to the Catholic Duke of Alençon in

The Discoverie of a Gaping Gulf whereinto England is like to be swallowed by another French marriage (1579). He fulminated against such a contrary coupling of good and evil. A proclamation was issued on 27 September that all copies of the book should be destroyed in the presence, or open sight, of a public officer. Camden was one of the spectators on 3 November when Stubbes made his appearance on the scaffold, or stage, to receive his punishment for offending the Queen. He records this particular spectacle of suffering in his *Annales*:

> Not long after upon a Stage set up in the market-place at *Westminster*, *Stubbes* and *Page* had their right hands cut off by the blow of a Butcher's knife, with a mallet struck through their wrists. . . . I can remember that standing by *John Stubbes*, so soon as his right hand was off, put off his hat with his left, and cried aloud, *God Save the Queen*. The people round about him stood mute, whether stricken with fear at the first sight of this strange kind of punishment, or for commiseration for the man whom they reputed honest, or out of a secret inward repining they had at this marriage, which they suspected would be dangerous to Religion. (Bk. 3, p. 16)

On the one hand, Stubbes performed the part that had been written for him to perfection. He endured his punishment and thanked the Queen for inflicting it upon him even though the executioner needed three blows to complete the task. On the other hand, however, this performance of loyalty may have conveyed a very different message. The act of immediately doffing his hat with his left hand, while his right hand lay on the floor of the stage, could have been seen as one of defiance rather than deference. The spectators could have appeared as though they were playing the parts that had been written for them in the official script by being deeply affected by this particular outward show. Camden suggests, nevertheless, that the relationship between the 'inward' feelings of the spectators and their own outward show of conformity was not necessarily as straightforward as Elizabeth would have liked. Their performance was also a mixture of defiance and deference. Stubbes, who probably fainted after raising his hat, was taken back to prison and held there for two years.

Michel Foucault's analysis of 'The Spectacle of the Scaffold' in *Discipline and Punish: The Birth of the Prison* (1977 edition) draws attention to some of the problems that could occur when there were competing interpretations of public punishments. He suggests that they were not eventually stopped out of humanitarian concern, but rather because there were doubts about whether such displays of power fulfilled their function of coercing all of the spectators all of the time. There is evidence that they produced disorder as well as order in Elizabethan England. A riot took place at Holborn in 1592 at the execution of somebody condemned for killing an unpopular official. A Renaissance execution was meant to represent what Foucault calls a theatre of Hell. Agony had to be prolonged for as long as possible so that both the victim and the spectators were given a glimpse of the everlasting torments associated with Hell. The point that an execution represented not an end but, rather, merely the prelude to endless torture was reinforced by the way in which the spectacle continued after the eventual death of the victim. Dismemberment of the corpse, followed either by the burning or display of its fragments, suggested that death offered no release from punishment.

The executioner himself had an ambiguous part to play in this theatre of Hell and was thus capable of disrupting the spectacle. He played Lucifer when he burnt and dismembered bodies. He was also one of the ruler's representatives on this particular political stage. As Foucault notices, executioners were given leave, or licence, to perform excessive acts of violence to demonstrate the power of their employers, which was capable of pursuing those who challenged it even after death. Pedringano comments briefly on the ambiguity of the executioner's status when he suggests in Thomas Kyd's *The Spanish Tragedy* (? 1585–7) that the Hangman is still a rogue even though he may hold an 'office' (2.7.81). There were still occasions when most members of a community helped out at an execution. There seem to have been plenty of willing pairs of hands to operate the guillotine that was used in Halifax. This was nevertheless an exception to the general rule that an executioner was an individual appointed to the office by the State. He could also be seen as a knave who did the Devil's work.

It was not just the events on the scaffold itself which were prolonged as part of this display of power. They were preceded by a slow procession from the prison to the place of execution. Halts were called at strategic places along the route so that the nature of both the offence and the punishment could be proclaimed. The condemned person was also allowed to show signs of repentance to the crowds that lined the streets. The practice in France was to gag those considered to be heretics, whereas in England they were almost always given opportunities to confess the error of their ways. The main features of the procession were then re-enacted for the benefit of the spectators who had managed to get close to the scaffold. Proclamations and confessions had to be delivered before the executioner could begin the slow process of death by torture. Witnesses were sometimes produced to give their versions of the crime. It was customary for the condemned person to forgive the executioner for the brutalities that he was about to inflict. This was meant to weaken the parallel that could be drawn between his activities and those of the Devil. Each part of this official script was in danger of producing meanings which could subvert the chastening, deterrent effects of the theatre of Hell. There was, for instance, no guarantee that the condemned person would perform the part as written. Parry retracted his confession and Stubbes's gesture of loyalty could also have carried a message of defiance. Pedringano, who is executed on stage, does not follow the official script and repent because he has been tricked into believing that there will be a last minute reprieve.

The main purpose of Foucault's account is to contrast the public spectacle of punishment with modern orthodoxies concerning the need to keep criminals under constant surveillance. He summarises the modern mentality as one that insists that 'punishments must be a school rather than a festival; an ever-open book rather than a ceremony' (p. 111). Modern punishments are designed to educate, or reform, the criminal rather than an audience which is made to watch him or her suffer. Their effect therefore has to be monitored by those trained in the various branches of human surveillance. Foucault's polarisation between spectacle and surveillance is in danger of underestimating their co-existence in the early modern period. Houses of correction placed an emphasis on surveillance and reform. The London Bridewell was established in 1553 and its regime was quickly copied in other major cities. Elizabethan prisons were certainly not constructed along modern, Benthamite lines and yet the eye of power was still present. It was Walsingham's spies, or eyes, working inside the prisons who helped to bring the Babington conspirators and others to the scaffold. Stubbes was publicly punished and then taken back to prison.

The executions of the Babington conspirators were spread out over two days. Savage, Ballard, Babington and four others were brought to the scaffold on 20 September 1586. This had been specially erected at St Giles in the Fields as this was one of the places where the conspiracy had been hatched. Although a large, permanent gallows had been erected outside the city at Tyburn in 1571, it was often felt that an execution achieved a more dramatic impact if it took place at a location that had an intimate connection with the crime. Pirates were taken from the Marshalsea and executed by the river at low tide. The authorities possessed at least one moveable gallows, which could be wheeled around the city so that executions could take place right outside a criminal's home. Processions made a point, if they could, of stopping at the scene of a crime before proceeding to the scaffold. Those convicted of wilful manslaughter sometimes had their right hands cut off near the scene of the crime, before being brought to the scaffold itself. The Babington conspirators were not alone in having a special scaffold erected for them. William Hacket stood in a cart in Cheapside on 16 July 1591 and proclaimed himself to be the Messiah. He prophesied that a terrible judgement would be visited upon the lewd city unless its inhabitants, including Elizabeth herself, acknowledged his claims. He was executed in the same place on 28 July before an exceptionally large and hostile crowd. He ordered God to rescue him immediately. He played the part of Marlowe's Tamburlaine by declaring that he would set fire to Heaven and tear God down, if he was not instantly obeyed.

As indicated, the first act in these political morality plays was the procession from the prison to the place of execution. It was another kind of Elizabethan street theatre. The seven conspirators were drawn on hurdles from the Tower of London to St Giles in the Fields. Ballard had a hurdle to himself, whereas the other conspirators were drawn to the scaffold in pairs. This form of transport was used for both practical and symbolic reasons. The hurdle usually prevented the prisoner's skull from being broken, as well as helping to provide a visual reminder that he or she had lost their human status by being placed below an animal. Such processions need to be contrasted with the high ceremony that was employed whenever the Queen moved about the city. The journey to the scaffold was a grotesque, or inverted, version of a Royal progress. *The Quenes Majesties Passage through the City of London to Westminster the day before her Coronation* (1559), which was probably written by Richard Mulcaster, describes just such an occasion of high ceremonial display and civic pageantry. Elizabeth's route was from the Tower of London through the City to Westminster. The Babington conspirators and Hacket were drawn along parts of the same route. Elizabeth rode through the streets in a chariot and was greeted with 'prayers, wishes, Welcomings, cries, tender words' (A2r). The Babington conspirators may have also been greeted with prayers, although tender words were probably few and far between. Elizabeth thanked her audience through both words and gestures:

> And on the other side her grace by holding up her hands, and merry countenance to such as stood far off, and most tender and gentle language to those that stood nigh to her grace, did declare herself no less thankfully to receive her peoples good will, than they lovingly offered it unto her. (A2r)

She halted at various places along the route to accept gifts. The city as a whole represented a 'stage wherein was shown the wonderful spectacle of a noble hearted princess toward her most loving people' (A2v). Several smaller stages were erected on this central stage to display historical and mythological pageants, which were often acted by children. Those who transgressed against Elizabeth's authority were forced to take part in a grotesque 'passage' through the streets.

Engravings of Renaissance executions suggest that it was common practice for each hurdle to be accompanied by at least one clergyman. His function was to remind the prisoner of the need for a full public confession. Catholics were also given every encouragement to make a dramatic, last minute conversion to the State Church. A character in George Whetstone's *The Censure of a Loyall Subject* (1587) notes that these executions attracted a large crowd:

> I cannot number the thousands, but by computation, there were able men enough, to give battle to a strong enemy: . . .

the whole multitude, without any sign of lamentation greedily beheld the spectacle from the first to the last. (A4v)

There is, perhaps, just a hint of anxiety about the size and strength of the crowd behind this orthodox representation of it. Engravings also indicate that the audience for an execution, although embracing the entire social range, was nevertheless quite carefully segregated according to rank. This also happened in the public theatres. Members of the Privy Council, who represented the monarch on such occasions, occupied the balconies or windows of adjacent houses. Edward Jones, who was executed on the second day, addressed himself directly to Sir Francis Knowles for help with his financial affairs. It seems likely, therefore, that there was a ceremonial procession to the place of execution by important figures like Knowles before the grotesque, or anti-procession, arrived on the scene. Elizabeth's power was heightened by the fact that she was both present at, and absent from, public executions. She was symbolically present in the forms of her Privy Council and her officers such as the executioner. Her literal absence nevertheless suggested qualities of omnipotent detachment.

It was customary for the scaffold itself to be guarded by soldiers, who probably also took part in the ceremonial procession. Their presence was a defensive measure designed to prevent the spectators from giving battle to the protectors rather than the enemies of the State. It was also a more symbolically aggressive display of power. The stage itself was usually rather cluttered, even before the process of dismembering began. It had to hold the executioner and his team, who were usually members of his family, as well as all their instruments. Space also had to be found for the representatives of the law and the State Church. Fires were lit on or near the scaffold. The cauldron, which was used for parboiling the bodily fragments so that they could be displayed for longer, was usually placed to the side of the main stage area. There was a period, from 1530 to 1547, when the law allowed cauldrons to be used to boil alive those convicted of poisoning but, by this time, they were only used after the execution had taken place. It is just possible that Marlowe's *The Jew of Malta* (?1589) refers to this earlier practice when Barabas, whose crimes include poisoning, is boiled alive. It will be argued later on in more detail that the executions that have such an important place in Marlowe's plays need to be related to the script for the spectacle of suffering. Time was allowed for each of the seven conspirators to make a full confession of guilt. Ballard lived up to his billing as the villain of the piece by refusing to ask for the Queen's forgiveness:

> He craved pardon and forgiveness of all persons, to whom his doing had been a scandal, and so made an end; making his prayers to himself in Latin, not asking her majesty forgiveness, otherwise than 'if he had offended'. (ST, p. 1156)

The scaffold was one of the few places where it was possible to perform Catholic rituals. Other locations included public theatres, embassies and, if the accounts are to be believed, prisons like the Marshalsea. These rituals may have provoked hostile reactions from Elizabethan spectators who might, like Hatton, have associated them with the diabolical. *The Censure of a Loyall Subject* was certainly not impressed by them. The open display, or outward show, of such rituals was nevertheless always capable of producing alternative interpretations. This is why members of the State Church were always on hand to dispute with anyone who departed from the official script. The authorities could not in the end prevent dialogues from taking place both on the scaffold and around it. They could, however, limit the damage and disruption that was caused. Abington did not get his tables in the courtroom and was unable to deliver his fighting talk on the scaffold without interruption:

> And being urged by Dr White to be of a lively faith; he answered, he believed steadfastly in the catholic faith. The Doctor asked him, how he meant, for I fear me, said he, thou deceivest thyself: he answered, That faith and religion which is holden almost in all Christendom, except here in England. This done, he willed them not to trouble him any longer with more questions, but made his prayers to himself in Latin. (ST, p. 1158)

Camden's account indicates that Tilney, who was also engaged in an angry exchange with Dr White, was pitied by the spectators.

This questions the version of audience reaction given by *The Censure of a Loyall Subject*. Titchbourne, whose speech from the scaffold was the most self-consciously rhetorical, also made a deep impression on the spectators according to all the acounts. *The Censure of a Loyall Subject* contradicts itself when it too comments on Titchbourne's favourable reception.

It was now time for the executioner himself to get in on the act:

> Ballard was first executed. He was cut down and bowelled with great cruelty while he was alive. Babington beheld Ballard's Execution without being in the least daunted: whilst the rest turned away their faces, and fell to prayers upon their knees. Babington being taken down from the gallows alive too, and ready to be cut up, he cried aloud several times in Latin, *Parce mihi, Domine Jesu!* Spare me, O Lord Jesus! Savage broke the rope, and fell down from the gallows, and was presently seized on by the executioner, his privities cut off, and his bowels taken out while he was alive. Barnwell, Titchbourne, Tilney and Abington were executed with equal cruelty. (ST, p. 1158)

It seems that nothing in Babington's life became him like the leaving of it. He had at last found a part he could play convincingly. It was that of a spectator. This account, graphic as it is in some respects, does not explain what the executioner did with the various bodily fragments. Such details were usually included in the sentence of death. The bowels were thrown onto the fire. The heart was ripped out and then also cast into the fire. The corpse was decapitated, the head held up to the spectators and then usually stuck on the top of the gallows. The 'privities' were then usually thrown into the cauldron. The remains of the seven bodies were then quartered. The limbs may have been parboiled in the cauldron by the scaffold, although they were probably put in baskets and taken to Newgate so that the job could be done properly. They were then displayed throughout the city to deter anyone else from imagining the death of Elizabeth, although they may well have prompted rather than suppressed thoughts on this subject. The executioner was usually allowed to keep what was left of a victim's clothes. He was under instructions on the second day of the executions to allow his victims to die on the gallows, before he started to dismember them.

This particular production of the theatre of Hell had its unscripted moments, for instance when Savage appeared to escape from the gallows. There was always a danger that the ceremony of execution would turn into black farce. The executioner obviously had to be able to improvise his part and yet it would still be dangerous to interpret his performance in terms of random butchery. He was a sacrificer as well as a butcher. His first target was what Mikhail Bakhtin describes in *Rabelais and his World* (1968 edition) as the lower, or grotesque, body. This assault on the bowels and 'privities' needs to be seen in terms of the classical body taking its revenge on the grotesque body. More specifically, the 'privities' were attacked to demonstrate that the condemned man had forfeited patriarchal rights of inheritance. Most of the Babington conspirators were able, when it suited them to do so, to offer the outward show of courtly bearing and posture. They were nearly all gentlemen. The executioner's task was to reveal the truth by openly displaying, to the victim as well as to the spectators, those parts of the body that were associated with rebellion and anarchy. He confronted the outward show, not just of courtliness but also of a more general humanity, with the inward realities. Witchcraft trials and related materials confirm that the grotesque body was specifically associated with Lucifer. The executioner was licensed to be demonic himself in order to combat the power of Hell.

Walsingham's theatre of rule was designed to display, or lay open, treasonable imaginations and practices which would otherwise have remained huddled up. The arrest of the conspirators became an occasion for public rejoicing. Elizabeth's letter to the Lord Mayor was read out to a large audience at the Guildhall and then published. The trials were concerned to display, rather than to establish, guilt. The conspirators were then exhibited in the streets as the anti-progress made its way to the scaffold. The executioner was licensed to lay open their bodies to reveal the grotesque realities that were hidden beneath a show of courtliness. The script nevertheless required that the parts played by Poley, Maude and 'the honest man' should stay huddled up. It also had no use for the incompetent watchmen of Enfield. There were times when those associated with the theatre of misrule played the parts that had been written for them. Some of the conspirators disguised themselves as labourers to avoid arrest. There were other times, however, when they seemed anxious to display rather than to huddle up their activities. Ballard almost advertised his presence by electing to act the part of flamboyant Captain Fortescue. Babington, Titchbourne and some of the other conspirators flaunted both themselves and their plans in the streets and taverns around the Inns of Court. It may, paradoxically, have been their desire to display themselves so openly that allowed Walsingham to produce the script in which they were cast as characters who huddled up high treason.

3
The Accidental Death of a Spy

3.1 I will have a bout with thee

Marlowe was still at university in 1586 and played no part in the drama of the Babington conspiracy. He may, however, have already been recruited to the secret service by this time to practise against Catholics in Cambridge. Robert Poley was to become one of his associates and, as will be seen, was present when he was killed in Deptford in 1593.

The instant success of the *Tamburlaine* plays in 1587 provoked hostile comments from Robert Greene. He accuses Marlowe in *Perimedes the Blacksmith* (1588) of making a hero out of an atheist. He adds the charge of being one of Niccolò Machiavelli's disciples in *Greene's Groatsworth of Wit* (1592):

> Is it pestilent Machiavellian policy that thou hast studied? . . . The broacher of this Diabolical Atheism is dead, and his life had never had the felicity he aimed at: but as he began in craft, lived in fear, and ended in despair. . . . and wilt thou my friend be his disciple? (CH, p. 30)

Greene, now desperately trying to play out his own final scene as a reformed sinner, casts the more successful Marlowe in the role of the Devil's disciple. Athough he was confined to his squalid lodgings by both illness and poverty, writing allowed him to stage a series of rhetorical bouts in which he always had the last word.

Ralegh was still the Queen's favourite when Marlowe took London by storm. As Captain of the Guard, he was personally responsible for protecting her from regicides. He had made his entrance at the very end of the Babington conspiracy when he was given most of Babington's lands and goods. He was not only the perfect courtier, but also held court over a distinguished group of Renaissance intellectuals. This School of Night was dedicated to the conquest of new academic worlds. Many of its members, Ralegh included, had a reputation for being unorthodox in their religious views. It is possible that Marlowe became involved with this circle shortly after his arrival in London.

One of the few things that is known for certain about Marlowe's life in London is that he fought a duel with a William Bradley. He was challenged by Bradley while he was walking in Hog Lane during the early afternoon of 18 September 1589, according to the reconstruction in Mark Eccles's *Christopher Marlowe in London* (1934). Bradley's quarrel appears to have been primarily with one of Marlowe's friends, Thomas Watson, who was another writer under the patronage of Thomas Walsingham. The origin of the dispute seems to have been a reckoning, or bill, which Bradley failed to pay to one of Watson's associates. Bradley, spoiling for a fight, started to work off his grievances on Marlowe when they met accidentally. This, at least, is the official version of the script. Hog Lane was a well-known location for duels, so the meeting might have been arranged. According to the script, Watson then entered and Bradley turned his attention to him instead: 'Art thou now come? Then I will have a bout with thee' (p. 10). Bradley was stabbed to death during this second bout. The duellists probably used the increasingly fashionable Italian weapons and techniques. Marlowe and Watson were arrested by the Constable of Norton Folgate and immediately entered a plea of self-defence. They were brought up before the Lieutenant of the Tower, who committed them to Newgate. It is not known whether they were placed in the worst part of the gaol, which was known as Limbo. Marlowe was eventually released on bail on 1 October, although Watson was forced to remain a prisoner until the case came up on 3 December. His plea of self-defence was accepted and yet he had to wait in prison until February 1590 for a Royal pardon.

Norton Folgate was one of the districts that were known as Liberties because they were beyond the jurisdiction and surveillance of the City of London. As Steven Mullaney suggests in *The Place of the Stage: License, Play and Power in Renaissance England* (1988), their marginality allowed them to become culturally central since they provided spaces and opportunities for dialogues with authority. The main public theatres of Marlowe's day, such as The Theatre (1576), The Curtain (1577) and The Rose (1587), were all built in these districts. The authorities were nervous of the mingling, murmuring spectators who idled away their time at these theatres. It was feared that both contagious diseases and ideas might spread amongst them unchecked. The Lord Mayor and Aldermen of London reiterated a series of familiar arguments when they petitioned to have the playhouses plucked down in 1597. The theatres are described as:

> the ordinary places for vagrant persons, masterless men, thieves, horse stealers, whoremongers, cozeners, conycatchers, contrivers of treason and other idle and dangerous persons to meet together and to make their matches, to the great displeasure of Almighty God & the hurt & annoyance of her Majesty's people, which cannot be prevented nor discovered by the Governors of the City, for that they are out of the City's jurisdiction. (E.K. Chambers, *The Elizabethan Stage* (1923, 4, p. 322)

The actors were seen as being just as dangerous as their audiences in such critiques of the theatre because they were marginal to a moral jurisdiction that emphasised patience, perseverance and, above all, constancy. They played too many parts. The toe of the peasant actor was often seen to be inside the shoe of the courtier. The convention of using male actors, or 'playboys', to act the woman's part meant that there was a danger of sexual as well as social anarchy. Actors sought protection from the hostility that they, like their customers, attracted for being masterless men by associating themselves with members of the aristocracy. Marlowe's plays were acted by the Lord Admiral's Men, Lord Strange's Men and Lord Pembroke's Men. Aristocratic patronage, together with living and working in the Liberties, minimised the risk of political interference and maximised the possibilities for dialogue.

It was not just Puritans who campaigned against the public theatres. Stephen Gosson was an Anglican clergyman who had, like Marlowe, been a scholar at the King's School in Canterbury. He engaged in bouts with Puritans as well as with actors, probably because they both competed with him for audiences. He was also involved with the secret service and one of his critiques of theatre and theatricality, *Plays Confuted in Five Actions* (1582), was dedicated without irony to Walsingham. It seems that he may have been insinuated into the English College at Rome. He made great play in *The School of Abuse* (1579) of the way in which theatres were market places for a whole series of bawdy transactions and exchanges, between actors and spectators, as well as between the spectators themselves. It was not just a case of theatres providing locations for generalised forms of sexual licence or liberty. Gosson and others expressed more particular anxieties about the ways in which theatres were breeding grounds for what they took to be effeminacy. John Rainoldes, who was closer to the Puritan tradition, refused to accept that there could be any exceptions to Old Testament rules against cross-dressing. Both actors and spectators were in danger of losing their identities when men dressed as women. *Th'Overthrow of Stage-Playes* (1599) is Rainoldes's version of his dispute with William Gager on the subject. Their argument, or bout, concentrates upon university rather than public theatre. Rainoldes, in common with other writers against the theatre, makes a highly theatrical critique of theatricality. He likens himself at one point to a public executioner who chops off the heads, or headings, used by his opponent and then displays them to the spectators:

> Moreover, as in beheading of noble personages, that are traitors, the executioner, having cut off their heads, doeth hold them up in his hands, & shew them to the people: so I, having thus beheaded, as it were, these of your six examples. . . might hold them up in my hands, and show that they are dead. . . . (p. 89)

Rainoldes is convinced that the theatre is the Devil's work and stages his own version of the theatre of Hell in order to overthrow it. His critique of theatricality is often a celebration of it.

Marlowe continued to combine espionage with writing after leaving Cambridge. Sir Robert Sidney, the Governor of Flushing, wrote to Burghley on 26 January 1592 to provide some background on the prisoners whom he was shipping back to England:

> I have also given in charge to this bearer my ancient two other prisoners, the one named Christopher Marly, by his profession a scholar, and the other Gifford Gilbert a goldsmith taken here for coining. . . The matter was revealed unto me the day after it was done, by one Ri:(chard) Baines.

Baines seems to have been a Cambridge graduate who had been insinuated into the seminary at Rheims. It appears, from the rest of this letter, that he and Marlowe may have quarrelled while on an operation in Flushing. Sidney described how Baines:

> was their chamber fellow and fearing the success, made me acquainted with all. The men being examined apart never denied anything, only protesting that what was done was only to see the Goldsmith's cunning: and truly I am of the opinion that the poor man was only brought in under that colour, what ever intent the other two had at that time. And indeed they do one accuse another to have been the inducers of him, and to have intended to practice it hereafter: and have as it were justified him unto me.

It seems that, initially, Marlowe and Baines were involved in the standard secret service practice of giving out that they were interested in illegal activities in order to trap those engaged in them. They themselves were engaged in counterfeiting. One of the most persistent complaints against actors was that they counterfeited emotions and personalities. The critique was extended to characters in the stage-play world such as priests and soldiers. Baines appears to have parted company with Marlowe because he felt that his companion was more interested in committing rather than preventing treasonable crimes. Flushing had a reputation for producing counterfeit coins. When Robert Rive was arrested in Southwark in 1586 for using illegal coins, he admitted that he had got them from Flushing. Baines and Marlowe had a bout with each other and it was Baines who got to the Governor first. The specific accusation about counterfeiting became part of a wider quarrel about loyalty. According to the Governor, the two agents 'do also accuse one another of intent to go to the Enemy or to Rome, both as they say of malice one to another' (Wernham, pp. 344–5). Nothing serious happened to Marlowe as a result of this accusation which, once again, forced him to play the part of a prisoner. Baines was nevertheless waiting in the wings in 1593 to get his revenge by accusing Marlowe of even worse crimes.

3.2 Journal of a Plague Year

The plague became hotter during the course of the summer of 1593. It only started to cool down in the autumn. Theatres and most large fairs were closed down in the hope of preventing the spread of disease. As it was usual for about half of a person's plague sores and swellings to be concentrated in the area of the privities, the plague became linked with immorality. The brothels were frequently raided during an epidemic and prostitutes imprisoned. Some interpretations termed the plague as the scourge of God visited upon a lewd and licentious city, whereas others blamed a combination of bad blood and foul air.

The Elizabethans may not have diagnosed the cause of the disease correctly and yet their measures against it might have achieved greater success if they had been systematically enforced. The main task was to isolate plague victims. This was very occasionally done through establishing primitive pesthouses, or else through utilising some of the existing facilities for detention. Dekker's *The Wonderful Year* (1603) personifies the plague as a 'stalking' (p. 31) Tamburlaine who lays seige to the city from its margins. The comparison is apt since the plague, like Marlowe's scourging hero, caused some of its victims to be confined in cages. It was felt that these common cages, which were normally used for the display of criminals, were too overcrowded during the 1603 epidemic:

> The cages (both in the Liberties and Suburbs) are full of sick folks, and when they die, the straw thrown about the streets,

fresh straw put it, and new sick persons: I have often seen three in one cage together, and people continually about them. (F.P. Wilson, *The Plague in Shakespeare's London* (1963, p. 94)

The cages were used to confine, but also to display, those who had broken plague orders which sought to restrict movement. Plague victims were meant to remain at home for a minimum of twenty eight days with the possibility of the period being extended up to forty days. The sign of a cross was placed on the door and anyone who visited the house had to acknowledge such a contact by carrying a red wand in the streets. All those who posed a threat to Elizabethan society were required to make an outward show of the fact. Those who caught the plague were also plagued by corrupt officials and tradesmen, as well as by more straightforward looters and pillagers. Bribery as well as drunkenness reached epidemic proportions. Jonson's *The Alchemist* (1610) shows how members of the underworld came into their own during a plague year because many heads of household and other figures of authority fled from the city.

The streets resembled a version of the theatre of Hell. If the plague really was the scourge of God, then perhaps there was no point in trying to prevent it from spreading. Grotesque dances of death took place, which flouted the authorities who decreed that there should be no bodily contact. They were also a way of flouting, as well as courting, death itself. It was official policy for large numbers of dogs to be culled at the beginning of an epidemic, many of whom were left to rot in the streets. Human bodies tended to turn black as a result of the plague. They were given a burial of sorts: covered in a sack or sheet and dumped in a shallow common grave late at night. The plague pits, like the scaffold itself, were seen as Hell on earth. Demonic associations worried the authorities sufficiently for it to be decreed that burials should take place as soon as possible after sunset.

London was, according to many of its inhabitants, also visited with another plague in 1593. This was seen as taking the form of Protestant refugees fleeing from religious wars. This was also the year in which Ralegh was attempting to remove the Queen's displeasure at his marriage to Elizabeth Throckmorton through patriotic performances in Parliament. He pressed the case for subsidies to finance the struggle against Spain but was not convinced that alien strangers, even though many of them were also the enemies of Spain, ought to receive sympathetic treatment:

> Whereas as it is pretended, that for Strangers it is against Charity, against Honour, against profit to expel them; in my opinion it is no matter of *Charity* to relieve them. For first, such as fly hither have forsaken their own King; and Religion is no pretext for them, for we have no Dutchmen here, but such as come from those Princes where the Gospel is preached, and here they live disliking our Church. For *Honour*, it is Honour to use Strangers as we be used amongst Strangers; And it is a lightness in a Commonwealth, yea a baseness in a Nation to give a liberty to another Nation which we cannot receive again. (Sir Simonds D'Ewes (ed.), *A Compleat Journal* (1708, pp. 508–9).

He went on to argue that strangers could not be trusted because they placed profit before country. Similar accusations are made against Barabas in *The Jew of Malta*. Ralegh hoped that such patriotic statements might demonstrate his desire not to be a stranger to the Queen.

There were other demonstrations against alien strangers in London. Inflammatory writings appeared on church walls and elsewhere in the new immigrant communities. One of these attacks carried the signature of Tamburlaine. The authorities investigated a rumour that Thomas Kyd was involved. His rooms were searched on 12 May. He was taken to Bridewell when an unorthodox religious tract was discovered. He was probably tortured on the rack, which was another stage on which the conflict between the classical and grotesque body was acted out. Those who held grotesque opinions were given bodies to match. Kyd never recovered from this ordeal and died at the end of the following year. He laid the blame on Marlowe for the unorthodox tract that was found in his possession. He made connections between it and Marlowe's own religious views in letters to Sir John Puckering, the Lord Keeper, after his release from Bridewell. Puckering may have asked him to rack his brains for more precise details about Marlowe's opinions. Kyd remembers that Marlowe:

would report St John to be our Saviour Christ's Alexis I
cover it with reverence and trembling that is that Christ did
love him with an extraordinary love.

Kyd accuses Marlowe of stating that Christ was homosexual. He
goes on to recount Marlowe's mockery of both Saint Paul and the
parable of the prodigal son. He then points out that Marlowe
delighted in both verbally and physically abusing his companions.
He also suggests that Marlowe was a political traitor, who tried to
persuade 'men of quality' to abandon allegiance to Elizabeth in
favour of James (CH, pp. 32–6). Kyd takes such an outward show
of disloyalty very literally, although it was standard practice in the
secret service to give out that one was going to Rheims or Scotland
in order to gain confidences.

Kyd wrote to Puckering after Marlowe's death and this may
have been how he justified the character assassination to himself.
It is nevertheless quite likely that he bought his release from
Bridewell with at least a version of these charges against Marlowe.
He did this in the knowledge that even some of the minor
accusations could have cast Marlowe as a victim in the theatre of
Hell. The Star Chamber, probably acting on Kyd's information,
issued a warrant on 18 May ordering Marlowe to appear before it
as soon as possible. It was served on him at Scadbury, the
residence of Thomas Walsingham. The closure of the theatres,
together with the increasing heat of the plague, meant that it was
neither necessary nor safe for him to remain in London. Those
who stayed behind became increasingly hysterical about threats
from aliens. Archbishop Whitgift chose this moment to intensify
his crusade against Puritans. Henry Barrow and John Greenwood,
who had been in prison for six years for their attacks on bishops,
were suddenly executed on 6 April. John Penry was probably one
of the authors of the controversial *Marprelate Tracts* (1588–9),
which also attacked bishops or petty popes. He was quickly and
unexpectedly hanged on 29 May. Every effort was made to
prevent his supporters from finding out about the timing of the
execution in order to prevent crowd trouble. If Kyd is to be
believed, Marlowe's critique of the State Church was even more
radical than the one offered by these advanced Puritans. Ralegh
felt more sympathy for such groups than he did for alien strangers.

Although he declared in Parliament that a sect like the Brownists ought to be rooted out of the Commonwealth, he cleverly outlined some of the practical problems involved in doing so.

Marlowe appeared before the Star Chamber, presided over on this occasion by Whitgift, on 20 May:

> This day Christopher Marley of London, gentleman, being sent for by warrant from their Lordships, hath entered his appearance accordingly for his Indemnity therein, and is commanded to give his daily attendance on their Lordships until he shall be licensed to the contrary. (APC, 24, p. 244)

No further details are available. It may be that Marlowe, who had done Her Majesty good service over a number of years, was able to provide satisfactory answers to the accusations against him. Although the Star Chamber requested his 'daily attendance', this did not always have to be rigorously observed in practice. An alternative interpretation is that Marlowe was still under suspicion and put on strict probation while Kyd's allegations were investigated. Enter Baines. Although the exact status of his inquiries is unknown, his findings were eventually passed up as far as the Queen herself. There is some doubt, however, over whether they were received just before or just after Marlowe's death.

Baines's report, or libel as it is sometimes called, extends but does not fundamentally alter the terms of Kyd's character assassination. It may be that Kyd was one of Baines's sources. Marlowe is cast as a character who scoffs at the Biblical version of creation and ridicules accounts of Moses in the wilderness. He believes that the only function of religion is 'to keep men in awe' and endows Christ with human sexuality:

> That the woman of Samaria & her sister were whores & that Christ knew them dishonestly.
> That St John the Evangelist was bedfellow to Christ and leaned always in his bosom, that he used him as the sinners of Sodom.

Baines's Marlowe goes on to claim that 'all they that love not Tobacco & Boys were fools'. He flouts political authority by asserting that 'he had as good Right to Coin as the Queen of

England'. He not only holds monstrous opinions, but also tries to convert others to them. Richard Cholmley is named as a witness who could testify that Marlowe tried to persuade him to become an atheist. He was another member of the secret service who practised upon Catholics. The evidence suggests that he was prepared to let them escape if they paid him well enough. Perhaps Baines also had to pay him. Baines concludes that Marlowe ought to be silenced: 'I think all men in Christianity ought to endeavour that the mouth of so dangerous a member may be stopped' (CH, pp. 36–8). One of the punishments for blasphemy was for the offender's tongue to be cut out. Perhaps this is what Baines recommends, although his remarks can also be read as calling for Marlowe's death.

Alan Bray suggests in *Homosexuality in Renaissance England* (1982) that Baines's representation of Marlowe follows the conventions of Protestant propaganda. Marlowe's otherness is constructed in religious, political and sexual terms. The 'sodomite' was, by definition, also an atheist and political traitor. Bray nevertheless identifies a potential contradiction between this propaganda image of homosexuality and its social reality. Homosexual practices appear to have been institutionalised, and therefore to some extent normalised, in schools, universities and in the household itself. Bray prefers to explain discrepancies between image and reality not in terms of conscious toleration, but rather as a product of a more unconscious failure by members of society to make connections between the two. An important part of this argument concerns the way in which, propaganda aside, homosexuality was defined as being a specifically sexual practice rather than a wider social one. Bray suggests that it was the absence of an identifiable sub-culture which helps to explain the relatively limited number of prosecutions for homosexuality in the sixteenth and seventeenth centuries. These tended to occur either at times of social anxiety, or else as products of personal feuds. The plague year of 1593 was certainly a time of acute social tension and yet it still seems unlikely that Baines's employers would have paid specific attention to reports of Marlowe's homosexuality. A blasphemer was expected to be a political traitor and sexual deviant. Marlowe's *Edward II* (?1592), as will be seen, initiates a dialogue with authority by offering spectators a wider range of views on homosexuality.

Baines's report reveals a lot about the construction of propaganda. It has always been open to doubt how much it reveals about Marlowe himself. Those who are prepared to accept its evidence do so because they see it as being corroborated by Greene and, more particularly, by Kyd. It also appears to be backed up by some of the later accounts of Marlowe's death. Thomas Beard's *The Theatre of God's Judgements* (1597) reproduces similar stories about Marlowe's blasphemy:

> a playmaker, and a Poet of scurrility, who by giving too large a swing to his own wit, and suffering his lust to have full reins, fell (not without just desert) to that outrage and extremity, that he denied God and his Son Christ, and not only blasphemed the trinity, but also (as it is credibly reported) wrote books against it, affirming our Saviour to be but a deceiver, and *Moses* to be but a conjurer and seducer of the people, and the holy Bible to be but vaine and idle stories, and all religion but a device of policy. (CH, pp. 41–2)

Baines may well have got some of his information from Kyd, but Beard's sources remain a mystery. Some of the same details, for instance the remarks on Moses, occur in all three accounts. All three were nevertheless written from hostile points of view: Baines had fallen out with Marlowe in 1592 and Kyd was anxious to avoid the rack. Beard, like other Puritan writers, wanted to show that God was the only playwright whose works were fit to be watched.

3.3 The Reckoning

Marlowe did not make his 'daily attendance' before the Star Chamber on 30 May as he spent all day at Eleanor Bull's house in Deptford. Just as the Three Tuns had been one of the stages during the Babington conspiracy, so Eleanor Bull's house and gardens became a theatrical set in a related political drama. Some of the characters remained the same. Marlowe arrived at ten o'clock in the morning with three companions. Enter Poley, who had just landed from the Hague. He had been imprisoned in the Tower in 1586 which may have helped to maintain his cover. He went straight back to his secret service activities on his release. He undertook missions to Denmark, the Low Countries and France. He had also spent much of the earlier part of 1593 in Scotland. When he arrived at Deptford, he was carrying letters for his employers. These were not in fact delivered until 8 June. The record of this particular mission, which began on 8 May and ended on 8 June with the delivery of the letters, states that Poley was in Her Majesty's service for all of this time. The third character in the drama was Nicholas Skeres, another government agent who had had some shadowy involvement in the plot against the Babington plotters. The cast was completed by Ingram Friser, who was employed at Scadbury and is known to have been involved in shady business deals.

The four men were provided with food and drink. The Coroner's report, which is quoted in full in Leslie Hotson's *The Death of Christopher Marlowe* (1925), suggests that this was a business meeting rather than a social gathering. The morning was spent in discussions, which were followed by a meal. The four men spent the afternoon walking and talking in the garden and then went back to the house at six o'clock for another meal. If this was a business conference related to Poley's recent travels, then Marlowe's problems with the Star Chamber did not prevent him from continuing his intelligence activities. This is at least the impression conveyed by the outward show of events. The leisurely but secretive atmosphere changed after the evening meal. Marlowe and Friser had an argument over the bill, or what is referred to in the Coroner's report as 'the payment of the sum of pence, that is, le recknynge' (p. 32). Friser was apparently sitting between Poley and Skeres at a table with his back to Marlowe, who was lying on a bed. It seems that Marlowe struck Friser with the hilt of a dagger. The blade was therefore pointing towards him when Friser began to retaliate. Exit Marlowe. Friser entered a plea of self-defence which was accepted by the Coroner's jury. He went back to work immediately and received his pardon in just under a month. Poley continued to be employed by the secret service until the turn of the century when he appears to have lost favour. Skeres disappeared back into obscurity.

Many critics and biographers have tried to challenge this verdict of self-defence. Calvin Hoffman proposes in *The Murder of the Man who was Shakespeare* (1955) that Marlowe's death was a contrived legal fiction which allowed him to escape to Europe and therefore to elude the surveillance of the Star Chamber. The body that the Coroner examined was that of a drunken sailor. The staging of such an outward show certainly fits the theatrical style of the secret service. There is, however, no evidence to support the view that Marlowe survived to write the plays associated with Shakespeare while in forced exile. Hoffman is therefore reduced to producing passages from Shakespeare's plays that he claims have Marlowe's fingerprints all over them. The argument, based as it is on the snobbish assumption that only somebody who had had a university education could have written Shakespeare's plays, is not convincing.

Another way of challenging the verdict has been to suggest that Friser, Poley and Skeres were hitmen who were hired by somebody who wanted to stop Marlowe's dangerous mouth to prevent any incriminations. A number of characters have been cast for the role. Perhaps it was Ralegh, who feared that any detailed investigation of Marlowe's religious opinions would incriminate him and other members of the School of Night. His religious opinions were nevertheless the subject of an inquiry in 1594 and no action was taken against him. Perhaps it was Thomas Walsingham who feared guilt through association. There are many different theories and names, but common ground is provided by the fact that all the candidates are identified as individuals who believed that Marlowe might eventually betray them to the Queen's government.

The best candidate may, however, be somebody connected with government. Marlowe had been an agent for at least six years and so was privy to a number of State secrets. The evidence that was received, first from Kyd and then possibly from Baines, suggested that while he may have done her Majesty good service in the past his opinions rendered him a potential security risk. At the very least, he looked as though he might become an embarrassment. Those who accept Friser's plea of self-defence make great play of the fact that the meeting in Deptford passed amicably until after supper. If Friser, Poley and Skeres had orders to kill Marlowe, why did they wait so long to execute them? Such a straightforward line of questioning is not much help when trying to reconstruct the Machiavellian mentality of the Elizabethan secret service. The outward show of a friendly but important meeting which suddenly turned sour provided the necessary cover, or colour, by establishing that the secret service was not Marlowe's enemy. Alternatively, this meeting might have taken the form of a final de-briefing session. The accidental death of this spy may have been carefully stage-managed.

Part Two:

The Drama

4
Tamburlaine the Great:
Parts One and Two

4.1 Sights of Power

The Elizabethan Bridewells were established, as has been suggested, to reform prisoners. They therefore provide an important
qualification to Foucault's neat polarisation between spectacle
and surveillance. More specifically, the regime at the London
Bridewell developed into a complicated mixture of spectacle and
surveillance. Although it retained the original emphasis on correction, it was also used as a more conventional prison. Hacket spent
some time there after his arrest and Kyd was taken there to be
tortured. The punishment of masterless men and prostitutes often
took the form of both a school and a festival. As Dekker and
others indicate, the whipping of prostitutes could take place before
an audience. Other punishments required the prisoners to be
paraded through the streets. They were, for instance, escorted out
of Bridewell on a regular basis to clear the sewage from the
neighbouring streets. An account of this more public part of their
punishment, which was published in 1629 and is quoted in E. D.
Pendry's *Elizabethan Prisons and Prison Scenes* (1974), describes
how they piled 'Dirt and Dung' (I, p. 41) into a cart under the
direction of the beadles. Some of them pulled the cart through the
streets, while others had the task of filling it up. Those who pulled

may have been yoked together like horses. The beadles probably whipped them as if they were horses. This punishment provided a spectacle of suffering for those who happened to be in the streets at the time. The spectators appear to have been in a festive mood when they greeted the appearance of the dungcart with one of Tamburlaine's most notorious lines, 'Holla, ye pamper'd jades of Asia' (4.3.1).

The spectators were drawing on memories of Tamburlaine's dramatic entrance towards the end of Part Two of *Tamburlaine the Great* with his chariot being pulled by the Kings of Trebizon and Soria. The stage directions indicate that he holds the reins in his left hand, leaving his right hand free to scourge the kings with his wire whip. He thus stages a highly visual display of his power over the recently defeated kings. Those who greeted the dungcart may simply have been displaying their own power over the prisoners. They may, alternatively, have been offering a critique of such displays of power by equating the tyranny of the beadles with that of Tamburlaine. The actors in this piece of street theatre may or may not have been flattered to be associated with either Tamburlaine or the Kings of Asia.

The fact that an entrance from one of the *Tamburlaine* plays was still being recalled over forty years after their first performances is just one of the many examples that can be quoted to illustrate their truly phenomenal popularity. Two other examples have already been cited earlier on: Dekker's representation of the plague as a 'stalking' Tamburlaine and the denunciation of alien strangers in 1593 that claimed to have been written by Tamburlaine. He symbolises a disease and yet is also seen as the cure to a social malady. His position within the cultural memory was therefore an ambiguous one. It has also been suggested that Hacket's performance on the scaffold in 1591 may have owed something to Tamburlaine's reputation for daring gods out of Heaven. Further examples that could be added to the list include Pistol's garbled version of the 'jades of Asia' speech in Shakespeare's *2 Henry IV* (1597–8). The *Tamburlaine* plays became proverbial for their popularity and were frequently parodied. The success of Part One, which was probably first performed in 1587 led to the appearance, probably within the space of a few months, of Part Two.

The spectators outside Bridewell recalled a particular entrance. Both plays are characterised by memorable entrances and progresses, or passages, across the stage. The theatrical power of such moments is heightened not just by mighty lines of blank verse, but also by the use of props such as the chariot and the whip. As will become more apparent, the stage directions within the text itself also indicate the importance of costumes in helping to create a spectacular series of entrances and progresses.

There is a moment almost at the end of Part One which exhibits many of these distinctive features. It begins with an entrance. Tamburlaine and his followers, dressed in armour, lead the Soldan of Egypt on to the stage after they have defeated him in battle. The Soldan is, however, spared the ritual humiliation that is meted out to the 'jades of Asia' and others. This is because he is the father of Zenocrate, whom Tamburlaine wishes to marry. The stage is littered with corpses even though the battle has not taken place there. The King of Arabia was wounded in the battle and came on-stage to die. This happens after the captured Turkish Emperor, Bajazeth, and his wife, Zabina, have seized the opportunity to commit suicide on-stage.

Tamburlaine himself does not appear to see these corpses until he is at least half way through a long speech designed to affirm to himself and the Soldan that he is now 'the general of the world' (5.1.449). When he does at last notice them, he nevertheless effortlessly incorporates their presence into the rhetorical elaboration on his martial exploits:

And see, my lord, a sight of strange import,
Emperors and kings lie breathless at my feet;
The Turk and his great empress, as it seems,
Left to themselves while we were at the fight,
Have desperately despatch'd their slavish lives;
With them Arabia, too, hath left his life:
All sights of power to grace my victory.
And such are objects fit for Tamburlaine,
Wherein as in a mirror may be seen
His honour, that consists in shedding blood
When men presume to manage arms with him. (5.1. 466–76)

Tamburlaine colonises the stage and everything on it. The corpses are instantly transformed, as far as the Soldan is concerned, from a 'strange' sight into an ordered, harmonious one that reflects

Tamburlaine's power. The plays are characterised not only by dramatic entrances such as Tamburlaine's triumphant procession from the battlefield but also, more specifically, by the ways in which they allow Tamburlaine to stage a whole series of broadly similar 'sights of power'.

It is, however, almost as difficult to reconstruct how Tamburlaine's colonisation of the stage might have been received by Elizabethan audiences as it is to recover reactions to the appearance of the Bridewell dungcart. He might have been condemned for his failure to see beyond himself, just as he might have been applauded for the way in which his quick improvisation re-affirms his control of the stage. Such difficulties are also a distinctive feature of the plays.

4.2 That Sturdy Scythian Thief

Tamburlaine's enemies represent him as being, amongst other things, a 'thief' (1.1.36), a 'slave' (3.3.68) and a 'sturdy felon' (4.3.12). According to the Soldan, he commands 'a troop of thieves and vagabonds' (4.1.6). He is held to be a masterless man who haunts the margins and borders of civilised society. The plays nevertheless allow this alien stranger to capture and hold the centre of the stage. Such a provocative movement from the margins to the centre also takes place, as will be seen, in *The Jew of Malta*.

Tamburlaine's first appearance seems to confirm the demonology of his enemies as he has just ambushed Zenocrate and her followers. He may behave like a thief and yet he sounds like a Renaissance prince delivering a monologue of power. He remains totally unimpressed by the letters of safe conduct that Zenocrate is carrying. He does not see them because they do not mirror his power:

> But now you see these letters and commands
> Are countermanded by a greater man,
> And through my provinces you must expect
> Letters of conduct from my mightiness,
> If you intend to keep your treasure safe. (1.2. 21–5)

The discrepancies between Tamburlaine's appearance and his rhetoric, which unsettle Zenocrate and probably many spectators as well, do not last for long since he changes into a suit of armour:

> Lie here, ye weeds that I disdain to wear!
> This complete armour and this curtle-axe
> Are adjuncts more beseeming Tamburlaine. (1.2. 41–3)

Although some critics suggest that he throws off his 'weeds' to reveal that he is wearing armour underneath them, there is nothing in the text itself to support this reading. As his body and its proportions are a 'sight of power' and are quite frequently discussed as such, it is probably important that they should be displayed early on in the play. This would happen if he changed on the stage into the armour that had belonged to one of the captured lords. Renaissance moralists claimed that borrowed clothes never fitted properly and so were able to maintain hierarchical distinctions between the centre and its margins. Shakespeare draws on this tradition, without necessarily endorsing it, by suggesting that Macbeth may be dwarfed by the borrowed robes of kingship. The sight of Tamburlaine's costume change on the Elizabethan stage may have set up traditional expectations that such pride would inevitably lead to a fall. They are nevertheless not fulfilled as the armour turns out to be a perfect fit.

As noted, Elizabethan polemics against actors claimed that they were masterless men who threatened social hierarchies by insisting on playing the parts of kings and lords. This is exactly what the vagabond Tamburlaine does when he disdains to wear the costume, or badge, that society deems appropriate for his status. He is the peasant actor who puts his toes in the shoes of the prince or, more precisely, the shepherd who thinks it is more 'beseeming' to wear a splendid suit of armour. This scene can therefore be seen as playing out, in a provocative and confrontational manner, the fears that were associated with theatre and theatricality. Just as *Doctor Faustus* (?1592) often celebrates associations between theatricality and Hell, so this scene appears to take festive pleasure in throwing the anxieties of those who wanted to pluck down the theatres back at them.

Tamburlaine is an alien stranger in a more specific sense because of his Scythian origins, which are announced in the full title for Part One. Sir Antony Sherley describes the nomadic Scythians in his *Relation of his Travels into Persia* (1613) as 'being a people given to spoil, unquiet, and which cannot live in rest' (pp. 32–3). He accuses the historical Tamburlaine of destroying Persia and claims that his followers were the 'scum of Nations' (p. 41). Sherley was a supporter of the Earl of Essex who fashioned himself into a roving, freelance ambassador. His activities annoyed Elizabeth and her councillors because they often conflicted with government policy. He eventually became a Catholic and allied himself with Spain. He travelled to Persia in 1598 and so is using his retrospective account as a stage on which he can play the part of a great man who has honour in every country except his own. His hostility towards Scythians is endorsed by those who presume to manage arms with Marlowe's Tamburlaine. The Soldan sees Tamburlaine and his Scythian troops as representing the forces of anarchy:

> A monster of five hundred thousand heads,
> Compact of rapine, piracy, and spoil,
> The scum of men, the hate and scourge of god,
> Raves in Egyptia, and annoyeth us. (4.3.7–10)

The play allows Elizabethan anxieties about rebellion to be articulated around the figure of the Scythian.

Earlier writings establish the basis for Sherley's representations of the Scythians. Camden suggests that the native Irish might have had Scythian origins. This theory is developed by Irenius in Edmund Spencer's *A View of the Present State of Ireland*, which was probably written around 1596 although not published until 1633. He claims that the Scythians established themselves and their nomadic customs in the northern part of Ireland. They are held responsible for the introduction of long mantles, or cloaks, which are seen as being ideal garments for thieves. Perhaps Tamburlaine the shepherd exchanges a similar garment for his suit of armour. Irenius believes that Scythianism has to be destroyed root and branch. He proposes that any member of this wandering tribe who does not submit totally to colonial rule should be starved to death. This modest proposal is accompanied by plans for the confiscation of land, the transportation of any remaining Scythians from their homelands and the imposition of martial law. Irenius claims that the native Irish are nomadic, not just because they follow their flocks and herds, but also in every other aspect of their lives. They show no respect for settled allegiances, laws or sexual relationships. They are by nature restless. The brutes therefore have to be exterminated.

Irenius legitimates the conduct of some of the earlier colonists whose own restlessness brought them to Ireland before they moved on to the Americas. Ralegh's half-brother, Sir Humphrey Gilbert, was responsible for maintaining new English rule in Munster in 1569–70. Munster was often rendered as Monster in Elizabethan spelling. He blamed the troubles on the fact that the native Irish wanted their own monarchs and therefore were not prepared to offer allegiance to Elizabeth. He would appear before a castle and demand that it was surrendered immediately. If this was not done, he refused to accept a later surrender and put the whole garrison including women and children to the sword. He played the part of Tamburlaine before it was written. After a siege or battle, he lined up the heads of his victims outside his tent to provide himself and others with a memorable sight of his own power. They were the mirror that reflected his own martial power. The terror of his name alone opened many a castle gate. There is, as may have been noticed, some confusion about how Marlowe's Tamburlaine can be read in the context of these colonial narratives. He can be seen as being a representation of both the colonists and the colonised. It is a confusion that the plays do not resolve.

Ralegh himself served in Ireland between 1580 and 1581. He bombarded both Dublin and London with plans for destroying the wandering tribes, which included pleas for a return of Gilbert's reign of terror. Ireland became a stage on which he played, and was seen to play, his patriotic part. Although he was only a captain, he made sure that Burghley, Walsingham and other important figures registered both his presence and his views on the present state of Ireland. He fashioned himself into an expert on Ireland and was consulted as such after his return to England. His brief experience of subjugating the margins of Elizabeth's kingdom allowed him to become a more central figure at her court. He was remarkably skilful at making sure that his daring deeds figured prominently in contemporary accounts. The dashing captain became the hero of John Hooker's story of the Elizabethan colonisation of Ireland, which appeared in the sixth volume of

Raphael Holinshed's *Chronicles of England, Scotland and Ireland* (1587). He inserted stories about fighting off ambushes and bringing prisoners back through bandit country against all the odds. Hooker's narrative anticipates many of Irenius's objections to Scythianism, which is seen as producing 'great swarms and clusters of the idlers, which like wasps troubled the whole land, and lived only by spoil and rapine' (HC, 6, p. 381). He dutifully records how his dashing hero ordered one of these 'idlers' to be executed without trial for stealing firewood from his camp. Most Elizabethan writers on Ireland were obsessed by the dangers posed by swarms of masterless men. The existence of martial law saved the expense of establishing Bridewells.

Ralegh played an important part at the siege of Smerwick in the autumn of 1580. A mercenary army funded by the Pope landed at this fort on the south-west coast in the hope of joining forces with those who opposed new English rule. It was nevertheless trapped inside by the rapid advance of the English army under the command of Lord Grey de Wilton. The fort was then bombarded from both land and sea. The mercenaries decided to surrender in the hope that Grey would spare their lives. It is not clear whether he actually promised them safe conduct. The evidence suggests that he probably demanded an unconditional surrender. He nevertheless kept some twenty of the 'best sort' prisoners so that they could be ransomed by his officers. Elizabeth saw this as an infringement upon her prerogative to determine whether justice should display terror or mercy. Grey ordered the rest of the inhabitants of the fort to be killed on 10 November. The women and native Irish were executed in front of the fort. Ralegh and Captain Macworth were then put in charge of killing roughly six hundred unarmed mercenaries, sometimes referred to in the documents as strangers, who remained inside the fort. It took them and their soldiers about an hour to complete the task. The three members of the garrison who had been taken to a neighbouring blacksmith's forge to be tortured for information were finally executed two days later. Spencer, who may have been present at Smerwick since he was Grey's secretary, argued that his master had taken the only decision that was possible in the circumstances. Burghley's *The Execution of Justice in England* supports this view. The mercenaries are represented as rats who attempted to creep stealthily into the kingdom.

Hooker and the other writers who supported Elizabethan colonial policies sought to fix, or determine, the fundamental differences between the civilised and the wandering tribes. The Irish were demonised either for their Scythianism, or else because of their Catholicism. Barnaby Rich had been, like both Gilbert and Ralegh, an 'officer of the field' in Ireland in Elizabeth's reign. He argues in his *A New Description of Ireland* (1610) that the country was potentially ungovernable because its wandering tribes had been 'nuzzled from their cradles in the very puddle of Popery' (p. 15). Scythians were 'scum' and Catholics came from the 'puddle'. Once such fundamental differences were fixed, then events like the massacre at Smerwick required little justification. The colonial discourse can nevertheless be seen as fixing, or falsifying, differences. New English colonists like Gilbert and Ralegh were themselves restless, wandering adventurers from the same tribe who, because of their relatively obscure backgrounds, needed to establish both their fortunes and reputations in Ireland. They may have worn armour and despised Scythian costumes and customs, but they were also members of a rapacious wandering tribe.

The *Tamburlaine* plays have often been associated with Elizabethan colonial expansion, although the appropriate context has been taken to be the Americas rather than Ireland. It is nevertheless dangerous to see them as just promoting Elizabethan dreams of empire. Such dreams are disturbed by the presence of Tamburlaine himself. He casts off his Scythian 'weeds', puts on a suit of armour and then sets about colonising the world using many of Gilbert's tactics. It is as if a person pulling the Bridewell dungcart suddenly becomes the beadle in charge of it.

4.3 The Slippery Crown

Tamburlaine's rise to power is usually at the expense of a series of legitimate rulers. Might is shown to triumph over right. The first play chronicles the way in which he seizes the Persian crown, defeats the Turkish Emperor and triumphs over the Soldan. The odds against him appear to increase throughout the play and yet each time he overcomes them. Spectators who want to be assured that pride must go before a fall, and that borrowed clothes never fit, are doomed to disappointment. Tamburlaine merely goes from strength to strength. He both reaches and grasps what he desires. No threshold is of force to brave his entry.

The legitimate rulers whom Tamburlaine defeats command little respect. Mycetes, the Persian King, wants power without responsibility. He is therefore quite content to abdicate onerous duties to his brother:

> Brother Cosroe, I find myself aggriev'd,
> Yet insufficient to express the same,
> For it requires a great and thund'ring speech.
> Good brother, tell the cause unto my lords;
> I know you have a better wit than I. (1.1.1–4)

Cosroe delivers 'a great and thund'ring speech', although it is one that savages rather than supports the weak king. Mycetes is abused and mocked to his face and yet is powerless to do anything about it. The speech against Tamburlaine is eventually delivered by Meander, a court official. As Mycetes is so conspicuously unable to find a rhetoric that matches his position, his briefing to the captain who has been given the job of exterminating the Scythian thief becomes highly ironic:

> Go, stout Theridamas, thy words are swords,
> And with thy looks thou conquerest all thy foes. (1.1.74–5)

Mycetes himself neither looks nor sounds like a king. When he attempts to talk about his 'royal seat' (1.1.97), Cosroe impolitely suggests that he should kiss it.

Cosroe has in fact already made plans to depose his weak brother. Tamburlaine is not the first character to steal a slippery crown. The Persian lords offer Cosroe the crown together with plausible reasons for accepting it. It would benefit both the 'commons' (1.1.138) and the army. Mortimer employs the same arguments against legitimacy in *Edward II*. Like Mortimer, Cosroe stages a public performance in which he allows himself to be persuaded to accept a crown that he is itching to wear:

> Well, since I see the state of Persia droop
> And languish in my brother's government,
> I willingly receive th' imperial crown,

And vow to wear it for my country's good,
In spite of them shall malice my estate. (1.1.155–9)

He clothes his naked desires with a rhetoric of duty and service.
Tamburlaine is much more open and straightforward. He wants
'an earthly crown' (2.7.29) because it provides the ultimate sight of
power.

Tamburlaine uses his own thundering voice against Mycetes. He
is outnumbered by Theridamas's force and so decides to 'play the
orator' (1.1.129) rather than the soldier:

> In thee, thou valiant man of Persia,
> I see the folly of thy emperor.
> Art thou but captain of a thousand horse,
> That by characters graven in thy brows,
> And by thy martial face and stout aspect,
> Deserv'st to have the leading of an host?
> Forsake thy king, and do but join with me,
> And we will triumph over all the world. (1.2.166–73)

Theridamas is persuaded by Tamburlaine's looks as well as by his
words to 'prove a traitor' (1.2.226) to Mycetes. Tamburlaine uses
Theridamas's body as a mirror in which he sees a sight of
Mycetes's powerlessness.

Mycetes is unable, once again, to play the part of the orator
when his troops are waiting to give battle to Cosroe's army. He
allows Meander to try to stir up a hatred of the rebels, who have
now been joined by Tamburlaine and Theridamas:

> This country swarms with vile outrageous men
> That live by rapine and by lawless spoil,
> Fit soldiers for the wicked Tamburlaine: . . . (2.2.22)

This fighting talk against the Scythians is similar to Hooker's
polemic against the native Irish. Tamburlaine and Mycetes eventually confront each other during the battle. The legitimate ruler
has sneaked away from the field in order to hide his crown. He
does not want it to make him an easy target. He prides himself on
his Machiavellian cunning but, as usual, reveals the opposite of
what he intends:

Therefore in policy I think it good
To hide it close; a goodly stratagem,
And far from any man that is a fool. (2.4.10–12)

The comedy increases when he is caught in the act by stalking
Tamburlaine. He plays a parody version of a strong king. Tamburlaine is ordered to kneel down, told about military etiquette and
threatened with execution if he speaks out of turn. He does not,
however, steal the crown at this moment:

Here, take it for a while; I lend it thee
Till I may see thee hemm'd with armed men;
Then shalt thou see me pull it from thy head.
Thou art no match for mighty Tamburlaine. (2.4.34–7)

He needs to wait until he can play a scene which will provide a
sight of his power for a larger audience. Like Elizabeth and her
councillors, he is an expert in the choreography of power. Unlike
them, he is a masterless man from the margins of society.

Mycetes is comically absurd when he tries to play the Machiavellian ruler. Cosroe may be more cunning than his witless brother
and yet he too is shown to lack 'policy'. He subscribes to the
colonial view of Tamburlaine as a thief, although thinks that he
can get away with the 'stratagem' of forming an alliance of
convenience with him. He therefore ignores Machiavelli's warnings against making friends with real, or potential, enemies.
Tamburlaine presents Cosroe with the Persian crown after the
battle. It is the thought of Cosroe being able to ride in triumph
through Persepolis that makes him change sides so quickly:

And ride in triumph through Persepolis!
Is it not brave to be a king, Techelles,
Usumcasane and Theridamas?
Is it not passing brave to be a king,
And ride in triumph through Persepolis? (2.5.50–4)

He imagines himself as the leading actor in this 'sight of power'
and then will have it so. The mapmaker's wife in Ralegh's
anecdote was only able to hold territory, and therefore become
like a queen, in her imagination. She also had to persuade her

husband to let her do this. Tamburlaine's imagination, by contrast, is a spur to action. Theridamas, the dashing captain, also imagines the pleasures of wearing a crown:

> A god is not so glorious as a king:
> I think the pleasure they enjoy in heaven
> Cannot compare with kingly joys in earth;
> To wear a crown enchas'd with pearl and gold,
> Whose virtues carry with it life and death;
> To ask and have, command and be obey'd;...(2.5.57–62)

Although he is initially reluctant to aspire to a crown himself, he nevertheless eventually becomes a king along with Techelles and Usumcasane.

Cosroe is wounded in battle and reflects upon the fickleness of Fortune in the orthodox manner of *The Mirror for Magistrates* (1559) before he dies:

> Barbarous and bloody Tamburlaine,
> Thus to deprive me of my crown and life!
> Treacherous and false Theridamas,
> Even at the morning of my happy state,
> Scare being seated in my royal throne,
> To work my downfall and untimely end! (2.7.1–6)

He becomes the second king to lose his crown. Tamburlaine crowns himself King of Persia. This may set up expectations that he will also be broken on Fortune's wheel. They are not, however, fulfilled.

Persia falls relatively easily to Tamburlaine because both Mycetes and Cosroe are, in their different ways, weak rulers. Bajazeth, the Turkish Emperor, appears to be a much more formidable opponent. He sends one of his followers to order Tamburlaine to back down from such unequal contest:

> Your men are valiant, but their number few,
> And cannot terrify his mighty host.
> My lord, the great commander of the world,
> Besides fifteen contributory kings,
> Hath now in arms ten thousand janizaries,

> Mounted on lusty Mauritanian steeds,
> Brought to the war by men of Tripoli;
> Two hundred thousand footmen that have serv'd
> In two set battles fought in Graecia; . . . (3.3.11–19)

Tamburlaine refuses to be daunted by the size of Bajazeth's army
and declares that, in his role as 'the scourge and wrath of god'
(3.3.44), he will defeat the Turks in order to liberate Christians.
Spectators who may have anxieties about Tamburlaine's wilful
rebellion against legitimacy are not presented with attractive, or
viable, alternatives to it. The legitimate King of Persia is a fool and
the Emperor of Turkey is the sworn enemy of Christendom.
Tamburlaine catalogues some of the cruelties inflicted upon
'Christian captives':

> Burdening their bodies with your heavy chains,
> And feeding them with thin and slender fare,
> That naked row about the Terrene sea,
> And when they chance to breathe and rest a space,
> Are punish'd with bastones so grievously
> That they lie panting on the galley's side,
> And strive for life at every stroke they give. (3.3.48–54)

Popular prejudices against cruel Turks are being endorsed. *The
Jew of Malta*, by contrast, suggests that Turks may be more
chivalrous than the Christians. Spectators are placed in a difficult
position by Tamburlaine's claim to be the scourge of God. They
have to decide whether his ends justify his means.
   Tamburlaine's battles take place off-stage. Those who want to
condemn him for cruelty do not actually see him kill anyone until
he stabs his eldest son towards the end of Part Two. The stage
itself is reserved for the preliminary verbal skirmishes, or rhetorical bouts, in which words are swords. Tamburlaine scores a
direct hit by refusing to address Bajazeth deferentially:

> Kings of Fez, Moroccus, and Argier,
> He calls me Bajazeth, whom you call lord!
> Note the presumption of this Scythian slave!
> I tell thee, villain, those that lead my horse

Have to their names titles of dignity;
And dar'st thou bluntly call me Bajazeth? (3.3.66–71)

Bajazeth confirms the account of Turkish cruelty by declaring that he will have Tamburlaine castrated and make his captains pull Zabina's chariot. It becomes harder for spectators to condemn Tamburlaine's own cruelty after such threats. Bajazeth's excessive, bloated pride precedes his fall. His defeat in the rhetorical bout is followed by his defeat in battle. Like Cosroe, he suddenly finds himself broken on Fortune's wheel. His crown passes to Tamburlaine.

Tamburlaine confines his defeated enemy to a cage. As noticed, cages were used in the streets of London to display those who had broken the plague regulations. They were also used for other criminals. It has been suggested that public executions were usually preceded by two processions. The first one involved the stately passage of dignitaries and troops to the scaffold. This was followed by the grotesque, or anti-procession, which brought the bodies of the condemned to the place of execution. Tamburlaine's triumphant entry after the battle uses the same choreography. He and his soldiers are followed by an anti-procession that includes Bajazeth's cage. Like the 'jades of Asia' entrance, this one is also accompanied by a memorable line. When the two processions have come to rest, Tamburlaine gives the order 'Bring out my footstool' (4.2.1). Perhaps spectators borrowed this line to either taunt or amuse the caged prisoners in London. Tamburlaine constructs a sight of power by stepping on Bajazeth's back in order to ascend his throne. The ritual humiliation is completed by the way in which he throws back some of the abusive terms, such as 'slave', which Bajazeth had used during the rhetorical battle:

Base villain, vassal, slave to Tamburlaine,
Unworthy to embrace or touch the ground
That bears the honour of my royal weight.
Stoop, villain, stoop! Stoop, for so he bids
That may command thee piecemeal to be torn,
Or scatter'd like the lofty cedar-trees
Struck with the voice of thund'ring Jupiter. (4.2.19–25)

Bajazeth declares that Tamburlaine will not be able to control
Fortune's wheel for ever:

> Great Tamburlaine, great in my overthrow,
> Ambitious pride shall make thee fall as low,
> For treading on the back of Bajazeth,
> That should be horsed on four mighty kings. (4.2.75–8)

Such words may have a prophetic ring to them, but they turn out
to be merely wishful thinking.

Bajazeth becomes a grotesque jester at Tamburlaine's court,
who is expected to put on a 'goodly show' (4.4.55). His curses
provide entertainment, as does the sight of him refusing to eat the
scraps from the banquet that are offered to him on the point of a
sword. The banquet takes place on the second day of the siege of
Damascus and provides the occasion for Tamburlaine's followers
to be crowned as kings. Tamburlaine's custom when besieging a
city was to wear white on the first day to indicate that he would
accept an unconditional surrender. He wore red, or scarlet, on the
second day to signify that the leaders would have to die. He
changed into black for the third day to symbolise the total
destruction that was about to take place. The Governor of
Damascus describes Tamburlaine as a 'god of war' (5.1.1) and yet
he still does not respond to the change of colours. He may be
gambling on relief arriving from the Soldan in the nick of time. He
may, however, believe that he is cunning enough to save the town
on his own. He stages a play in which the Virgins of the city plead
with Tamburlaine to spare it. He believes that Tamburlaine,
although now dressed in black, will nevertheless be moved by this
sight. Tamburlaine converts it into one of his own 'sights of
power'. He orders his horsemen to kill the Virgins and their
'slaughtered carcasses' (5.2.131) are then hung up on the walls of
the city. The inhabitants, like the mercenaries at Smerwick, are
then put to the sword.

Part Two, which will not be dealt with here in as much detail as
Part One, does not resolve the question of whether there might be
alternatives to Tamburlaine's theatre of rule. Orcanes, the King of
Natolia and leader of the Turks, makes peace in a highly ritualised
manner with Sigismund, the King of Hungary, so that he can
protect his borders against Tamburlaine. Their peace treaty is

sealed with eloquent rhetoric, extravagant symbolic gestures and a banquet. It nevertheless turns out to have been merely an expedient, unholy alliance between Christians and Turks. Sigismund is easily persuaded by his Machiavellian advisers that he ought to break his oath. When Tamburlaine changed sides and attacked Cosroe he made a point of advertising his intentions, so that he could not be accused of acting in a 'cowardly' (2.5.102) way. Sigismund, the Christian warrior, has no such scruples. He is nevertheless defeated by Orcanes, despite having the advantage of surprise. He sees this as a punishment from God for breaking his oath. Orcanes is eager to confirm such an interpretation because he had called on Christ before the battle to help him defeat the 'false Christians' (2.2.62). The idea that 'God hath thunder'd vengeance from on high' (2.3.2) is not, however, allowed to go unchallenged. One of Orcanes's Viceroys, Gazellus, is much more sceptical about the possibilities for divine intervention:

> 'Tis but the fortune of the wars, my lord,
> Whose power is often prov'd a miracle. (2.3.31–2)

The question of whether there has been divine intervention is, like most of the other questions in these plays, left unresolved. All that can be said is that Orcanes is remarkably unsuccessful the next time he requires intervention. He calls on the god of the underworld to haul Tamburlaine 'headlong to the lowest hell' (4.3.42) after he has been defeated in battle. There is a deafening silence. He ends up having to haul Tamburlaine's chariot.

It appears, at first sight, as though Callapine may emerge as a worthy opponent for Tamburlaine. He is the son of Bajazeth, whom Tamburlaine prevents from claiming his legitimate inheritance by keeping him prisoner. He initially gives the impression that he is a man of action who finds it difficult to play the orator:

> Ah, were I now but half so eloquent
> To paint in words what I'll perform in deeds,
> I know thou wouldst depart from hence with me. (1.2.9–11)

This speech is nevertheless merely the prologue to an eloquent word-picture of the pleasures of kingship, which are promised to the gaoler if he will prove a traitor and change sides. It may be

compared with Tamburlaine's successful wooing of Theridamas.
Callapine returns to take his rightful place at the head of the
Turkish armies. He vows to be revenged upon Tamburlaine,
whom he describes as the 'proud usurping king of Persia' (3.1.15).
Expectations are set up that Fortune will fight on his side:

> We shall not need to nourish any doubt,
> But that proud Fortune, who hath follow'd long
> The martial sword of mighty Tamburlaine,
> Will now retain her old inconstancy,
> And raise our honour to as high a pitch
> In this our strong and fortunate encounter; . . . (3.1.26–31)

He goes on to recruit 'heaven' (3.1.32) and 'Jove' (3.1.35) to his
side for good measure. They are all joined by 'Mahomet' (3.5.16)
who is inevitably just waiting for the right opportunity to destroy
Tamburlaine. It is a mighty host. It is nevertheless routed by
Tamburlaine, along with Callapine's massive earthly host. Callapine himself flees from the battlefield. His deeds prove in the
end to be much less eloquent than his working words. He
re-appears towards the end of the play with another massive army.
He still believes that the gods, particularly Mahomet, are on his
side, despite all the previous evidence to the contrary. This time he
runs away even before he gets to the battlefield. Tamburlaine is
dying, but the sight of him and his chariot is enough to ensure
victory. Mahomet appears, once again, to be silent.

The Governor of Damascus in Part One proves himself to be
another of the play's failed Machiavellians when the show that he
stages with the Virgins fails to impress Tamburlaine. The Governor of Babylon in Part Two also jeopardises the lives of those
under his rule. He appears, initially, to take a firm stand against
Tamburlaine despite entreaties from the citizens that he should
surrender. He is committed to the defence of his realm:

> Villians, cowards, traitors to our state,
> Fall to the earth, and pierce the pit of hell,
> That legions of tormenting spirits may vex
> Your slavish bosoms with continual pains!
> I care not, nor the town will never yield
> As long as any life is in my breast. (5.1.43–8)

It is not just the 'faint-hearted' (5.1.36) citizens who plead with him to surrender. Theridamas offers to break the conventions for the third day of siege. The Governor's own life will be spared, if he yields the city and therefore makes things easier for the besiegers. It is a good bargain, given that the walls have already been breached. The Governor nevertheless refuses to countenance it. Being in the gallery, he would have been literally looking down on Theridamas at this point on the Elizabethan stage. It may seem that, at long last, a character emerges who claims the high ground of principle by refusing a deal to save his own skin. Such expectations are nevertheless breached almost immediately. The city is taken and Tamburlaine orders all its inhabitants, including women and children, to be thrown into the lake to drown. The Governor responds defiantly, perhaps articulating the outraged feelings of many spectators:

> Vile monster, born of some infernal hag,
> And sent from hell to tyrannize on earth,
> Do all thy worst; nor death, nor Tamburlaine,
> Torture, or pain, can daunt my dreadless mind. (5.1.110–13)

Fear of death then suddenly prompts him to change his mind. He begs Tamburlaine to spare his life in return for the gold that he had hidden at the beginning of the siege. Tamburlaine finds out the precise spot where the gold is hidden and then orders the Governor to be executed just the same. It is not made easy for spectators to find an honourable character who opposes Tamburlaine.

The Governor is hung in chains on the city walls and then shot at with guns by Tamburlaine's followers. Most critics feel that Philip Gawdy is probably referring to this scene when he describes in a letter dated 16 November 1587 an accident that took place in one of the public theatres during a performance by the Lord Admiral's Men. Some are nevertheless troubled by the early date that this suggests for Part Two. Gawdy was not present when the accident occurred and was merely relaying gossip about it back home. He claims that one of the actors swerved and fired his gun into the audience, killing a pregnant woman and a child, as well as wounding a man. He comments:

How they will answer it I do not study unless their profession
were better, but in Christianity I am very sorry for the chance
but God his Judgements are not to be searched nor enquired
of at mans' hands. And yet I find by this an old proverb
verified there never comes more hurt than comes of fooling.
(*Letters of Philip Gawdy*, 1906, p. 23)

Just as Thomas Beard detects the hand of God in Marlowe's death
so Gawdy is unable, despite his qualifications, to resist the
conclusion that those who associate themselves with the theatre
always run the risk of divine punishment. The *Tamburlaine* plays,
by contrast, debate rather than assume the case for divine intervention. Traces of the same debate can be found in Marlowe's first
play, *Dido, Queen of Carthage*. The squabbling gods and god-
desses appear to control human destinies, although Dido herself
claims at one point that this might be a convenient fiction. Aeneas
may plead that he has to leave her because he has been commanded
to do so, but she declares that 'It is Aeneas calls Aeneas
hence' (5.1.132).

A crucial moment in this debate in *Tamburlaine the Great* occurs
immediately after the execution of the Governor. Most Renaissance rulers burnt books that they felt questioned their authority.
Copies of John Stubbes's *The Discoverie of a Gaping Gulf* were
burnt after they had been surrendered by their owners. Tamburlaine continues his crusade against the Turks by burning the Koran
and daring Mahomet to punish him for his blasphemy:

> Now Mahomet, if thou have any power,
> Come down thyself and work a miracle.
> Thou art not worth to be worshipped
> That suffers flames of fire to burn the writ
> Wherein the sum of thy religion rests. (5.2.185–9)

Nothing appears to happen and then a little later Tamburlaine
claims that he suddenly feels 'distemper'd' (5.2.216). A question is
therefore posed as to whether his illness is just a coincidence, or
whether it is the result of divine intervention. It would have been a
very difficult one for Elizabethan spectators to answer since
Tamburlaine makes it quite clear that he is acting as the 'scourge
of God'. If there has been intervention, then it can be interpreted

as being against Christianity. The question may be simplified by the appearance of Callapine. As noted, he claims that Mahomet is fighting on his side and then runs away yet again from Tamburlaine. Perhaps the onset of Tamburlaine's final illness is purely coincidental. This was certainly the answer that was suggested in the 1976 National Theatre production. Judith Weil adopts a more subtle approach in *Christopher Marlowe: Merlin's Prophet* (1977) when she suggests that the plays dramatise 'the fearful silence of the gods' (p. 114). This is not necessarily an unorthodox position. Ralegh emphasises in his *The History of the World* that human actors can never be sure of the exact nature of the divine script. Gawdy may detect the hand of God in the deaths of theatre spectators and yet even he acknowledges the problems involved in searching out divine motivation. The 'silence of the gods' does not necessarily mean that they are dead although, given the unresolved nature of Marlowe's texts, this is nevertheless one of the answers that can be supplied by spectators.

Elizabethans who imagined laying their hands on the slippery crown often found themselves in the hands of the public executioner. This is what happened to the Babington conspirators. Tamburlaine's rebellion against legitimacy has the added provocation of being led by a masterless man, who belongs to a despised wandering tribe. The plays appear to support this movement from the margins to the centre by refusing to allow the case for legitimacy to be made with any conviction. The apparent 'silence of the gods' may help to remove any divine sanctions against rebellion. Tamburlaine the rebel nevertheless becomes Tamburlaine the king. He fights battles, sacks cities and punishes anyone who stands in his way. The plays therefore offer an outrageous assault on the crown and all it represents at the same time as they provide a celebration of monarchical power.

4.4 The Woman's Part

Zenocrate is an Egyptian princess who is captured by Tamburlaine while travelling through Scythia. She initially voices the prejudices against Scythians that run throughout the two plays. She pleads with Tamburlaine 'not to enrich thy followers/ By lawless rapine from a silly maid' (1.2.9–10). Olympia expresses similar anxieties

when faced with the prospect of being captured by barbarous
Scythians in Part Two. Zenocrate nevertheless begins to find
another voice. She is not sure that Tamburlaine is as 'mean' (1.2.8)
as he appears to be and addresses him as 'my lord' (1.2.34). It is at
this point that he becomes a lord by exchanging his mantle for a
suit of armour.

Tamburlaine uses Zenocrate as he uses the suit of armour to
enhance the sight of his own power. She is a commodity which,
together with this armour, the gold and the captured lords, is put
on display to persuade Theridamas to become a traitor. Tamburlaine himself may take the centre of the stage and yet he makes
sure that Theridamas sees the mirrors that are carefully arranged
around it to reflect his power. He claims that these mirrors have
been sent by Jove:

> See how he rains down heaps of gold in showers,
> As if he meant to give my soldiers pay;
> And, as a sure and grounded argument
> That I shall be the monarch of the East,
> He sends this Soldan's daughter rich and brave,
> To be my queen and portly emperess. (1.2.182–7)

Zenocrate is being used as a stage-prop in much the same way as
the Governor of Damascus uses the Virgins, although she is not
allowed to speak.

Tamburlaine's dominating performance may be primarily designed and choreographed to woo Theridamas and yet it can also
be seen as part of his campaign to win Zenocrate. He begins this
particular campaign just before the arrival of Theridamas by
declaring his love not just to Zenocrate herself, but also to his own
followers and the captured lords. He needs an audience for
everything that he does, whether it be winning Mycetes's crown or
Zenocrate's love:

> Zenocrate, lovelier than the love of Jove,
> Brighter than is the silver Rhodope,
> Fairer than whitest snow on Scythian hills,
> Thy person is more worth to Tamburlaine
> Than the possession of the Persian crown,
> Which gracious stars have promis'd at my birth. (1.2.87–92)

She remains silent while he delivers this hymn to her virginity and purity. It is meant to ambush those spectators who believe that Scythians, or members of any other wandering tribe, are incapable of controlling their sexual desires. Both the Turks and the Egyptians are convinced that Zenocrate has become one of Tamburlaine's concubines. Such an assumption reveals more about their own sexual standards than it does about those of the Scythians. Subsequent events cast some doubt on whether Zenocrate is really more important to Tamburlaine than slippery crowns. She is a useful rung on the ladder to the Persian crown since her silent presence helps to persuade Theridamas to change sides. This may be why Tamburlaine decides that she needs to be 'flattered' (1.2.107).

A conflict starts to take place in Zenocrate's mind between a desire to be loyal to her father and a wish to prove herself worthy of Tamburlaine's love. It is a conflict about the identity of her lord and it makes her weak and sickly. Agydas, one of the lords who was ambushed with her, notices that she is troubled by 'unquiet fits' (3.2.2) and that her face has become 'wan and pale' (3.2.5). He plays the part of her absent father and tries to get her to return to the voice that declares that all Scythians are engaged in 'lawless rapine'. Her mental and physical turmoil is caused by the fact that the voice of the father is increasingly at odds with her own experience:

> Leave to wound me with these words
> And speak of Tamburlaine as he deserves.
> The entertainment we have had of him
> Is far from villainy or servitude,
> And might in noble minds be counted princely. (3.2.35–9)

Although she is a princess by birth, she is nevertheless moving towards a position in which deeds are more important than pedigree. Agydas persists with his critique of Tamburlaine by offering a forecast of what can be expected from any relationship with a Scythian soldier. It turns out to have some truth to it:

> How can you fancy one that looks so fierce,
> Only dispos'd to martial stratagems?
> Who, when he shall embrace you in his arms,

Will tell how many thousand men he slew;
And when you look for amorous discourse,
Will rattle forth his facts of war and blood,
Too harsh a subject for your dainty ears. (3.2.40–6)

Agydas makes the mistake of voicing these opinions while fierce Tamburlaine is eavesdropping on the scene. As already noticed, Mycetes declares that a warrior should be able to use both words and looks as swords. He knows the part even though he is unable to play it. Tamburlaine, by contrast, is able to look daggers at his enemies. Callapine runs away from such 'killing frowns' (3.3.91). Agydas stands his ground when confronted by an exceedingly wrathful Tamburlaine, but knows that there is no escape. He accepts a real dagger and commits suicide, after Tamburlaine has led Zenocrate lovingly from the stage.

Zenocrate and Zabina, together with their maids, are expected to continue the rhetorical bout when Tamburlaine and Bajazeth eventually exit for the battlefield. They wear the crowns of their respective lords. They are like ventriloquists' dummies who echo their masters' voices:

Zabina: Base concubine, must thou be plac'd by me
That am the empress of the mighty Turk?
Zenocrate: Disdainful Turkess and unreverent boss,
Call'st thou me concubine that am betroth'd
Unto the great and mighty Tamburlaine?
Zabina: To Tamburlaine, the great Tartarian thief!
Zenocrate: Thou wilt repent these lavish words of thine
When thy great basso-master and thyself
Must plead for mercy at his kingly feet,
And sue to me to be your advocate. (3.3.166–75)

The term 'boss' in this context probably means fat or bloated. There is, perhaps, another reference to Zabina's size at the banquet when Usumcasane suggests that Bajazeth should kill her in order to provide himself with a month's supply of food.

Zenocrate and Zabina continue to fight their lords' battles, and therefore each other, after Tamburlaine's victory. They may appear to be on opposing sides, as well as being physically very different. They nevertheless both suffer as a result of Tamburlaine's cruelty. Zabina is not put in the cage, although she is forced to become part of the grotesque procession by following along behind it. She joins Bajazeth in his curses against Tamburlaine. They call on Mahomet to intervene against Tamburlaine and yet nothing happens. The apparent silence of the gods drives Zabina to the brink of despair:

> Then is there left no Mahomet, no God,
> No fiend, no fortune, nor no hope of end
> To our infamous, monstrous slaveries?
> Gape earth, and let the fiends infernal view
> A hell as hopeless and as full of fear
> As are the blasted banks of Erebus,
> Where shaking ghosts with ever-howling groans
> Hover about the ugly ferryman
> To get a passage to Elysium! (5.1.238–46)

Bajazeth commits suicide first. He does not do so in the stoical, classical manner adopted by Agydas. He has no dagger and so hits his head repeatedly against the bars of the cage. When Zabina finds his body, it becomes a sight of Tamburlaine's unstoppable power in a world which the gods seem to have forgotten. Her language disintegrates as she prepares to run at the cage and beat out her own brains:

> The sun was down – streamers white, red, black, here, here, here! Fling the meat in his face. Tamburlaine, Tamburlaine! Let the soldiers be buried. Hell, death, Tamburlaine, hell! Make ready my coach, my chair, my jewels. I come, I come, I come, I come! (5.1.313–16).

These are, as already noticed, the mutilated bodies that Tamburlaine fails to see when he makes his triumphant entry after defeating the Soldan.

Zenocrate pleads unsuccessfully with Tamburlaine to spare the citizens of Damascus because they are her father's subjects. She has to settle for a promise that her father will not be slaughtered along with everybody else. Tamburlaine then returns to what appears to be the more important task of humiliating Bajazeth. He confirms his masculinity through this baiting of a defeated enemy, whereas he sees it as being threatened by Zenocrate's pleas for clemency. He muses on the subject while his soldiers are spearing the Virgins of Damascus. He represents the wretched Zenocrate, with her 'hair dishevell'd' and 'watery cheeks' (5.1.139), as being his most formidable opponent to date:

> There angels in their crystal armours fight
> A doubtful battle with my tempted thoughts
> For Egypt's freedom and the Soldan's life,
> His life that so consumes Zenocrate,
> Whose sorrows lay more siege unto my soul
> Than all my army to Damascus' walls;
> And neither Persian's sovereign nor the Turk
> Troubled my senses with conceit of foil
> So much by much as doth Zenocrate. (5.1.151–9)

He appears to have forgotten the request to spare the lives of the citizens as well as that of the Soldan. He considers definitions of beauty and in doing so reveals the real reason why he is so troubled by Zenocrate's request:

> But how unseemly is it for my sex,
> My discipline of arms and chivalry,
> My nature, and the terror of my name,
> To harbour thoughts effeminate and faint! (5.1.174–7)

tempted to embrace conventional notions of mercy & moderation

He believes that she will make him 'effeminate'. It is as if her flowing tears threaten to dissolve and engulf his masculinity. He is not just worried about being thought to be 'faint' or weak. He is also concerned that he will become a feigned, or counterfeit, man. The speech finds a place for a remarkably idealised version of beauty in the masculine scheme of things, although it is still subordinated to manly virtue. Tamburlaine's thoughts then immediately return to Bajazeth and the progress of the siege.

Zenocrate and her maid are the first to discover the bodies of Bajazeth and Zabina. Like Tamburlaine, she does not notice them at first, although this is because she is preoccupied with the horrors rather than the triumphs of war:

The streets strow'd with dissever'd joints of men,
And wounded bodies gasping yet for life;
But most accurs'd, to see the sun-bright troop
Of heavenly virgins and unspotted maids,
Whose looks might make the angry god of arms
To break his sword and mildly treat of love,
On horsemen's lances to be hoisted up,
And guiltlessly endure a cruel death. (5.1.320–7)

Such events take place off-stage while Tamburlaine wonders whether real soldiers should surrender to beauty. When Zenocrate finally sees the bodies, they become for her yet 'another bloody spectacle' (5.1.337) in this catalogue of carnage. Like Ralegh in pessimistic mood, she believes that Bajazeth's rapid fall illustrates the unpredictability of Fortune:

Those that are proud of fickle empery
And place their chiefest good in earthly pomp,
Behold the Turk and his great emperess!
Ah Tamburlaine my love, sweet Tamburlaine,
That fights for sceptres and for slippery crowns,
Behold the Turk and his great emperess! (5.1.350–5)

This orthodox view does not, however, go unchallenged. Zenocrate's maid declares that Tamburlaine will retain his control of Fortune's wheel for as long as he lives. Minor characters often have the major task of disputing traditional positions. Just as Gazellus tells Orcanes that divine intervention may be a fiction, so the maid points out to Zenocrate that it may not be necessary to live in constant fear of falling.

The ending of Part One is full of surprises, particularly for those who may still retain prejudices against Scythians. Zenocrate becomes Tamburlaine's queen rather than his concubine in a ceremony that provides another sight of his power. She remains seated while he crowns her. The sack of Damascus suggests that, hymns to beauty notwithstanding, he is steeped in blood so far that he will never be able to renounce war. Agydas's words of warning seem to have come to pass. Yet Tamburlaine calmly tells those followers whom he has helped to gain crowns that the fury of his sword has at last been calmed:

Cast off your armour, put on scarlet robes,
Mount up your royal places of estate,
Environed with troops of noblemen,
And there make laws to rule your provinces.
Hang up your weapons on Alcides' post,
For Tamburlaine takes truce with all the world. (5.1.522–7)

He even decrees that Bajazeth and Zabina should be given
honourable funerals. He still commands Fortune.

This ending, which upsets many of the expectations that have
been self-consciously manipulated by the play itself, is in turn
upset by the existence of Part Two. Tamburlaine's truce is over
and Zenocrate is back in the familiar position of pleading with him
to cast off his armour. She sits flanked by her three sons. The
virgin bride is now a proud mother. Tamburlaine, whose power
over her and others has always been signified by his mobility,
restlessly paces up and down making sure that this family grouping
mirrors his own importance. The spectre of effeminacy haunts him
once more:

> But yet methinks their looks are amorous,
> Not martial as the sons of Tamburlaine.
> Water and air, being symboliz'd in one,
> Argue their want of courage and of wit;
> Their hair as white as milk and soft as down,
> Which should be like the quills of porcupines,
> As black as jet, and hard as iron or steel,
> Bewrays they are too dainty for wars. (1.3.21–8)

The two youngest sons, Celebinus and Amyras, are desperate to
prove that they have the potential to become hard, fighting men.
The eldest son, Calyphas, nevertheless has no desire to look like a
porcupine:

> But while my brothers follow arms, my lord,
> Let me accompany my gracious mother,
> They are enough to conquer all the world,
> And you have won enough for me to keep. (1.3.65–8)

Tamburlaine is furious and claims that only those who are prepared to 'wade up to the chin in blood' (1.3.84) are worthy to be called his sons. He waged war against the hereditary principle in Part One and, though he has now founded his own dynasty, is prepared to disinherit his eldest son. He still maintains that crowns should only be worn by those whose deeds render them worthy to do so.

Zenocrate becomes a lady whom time hath surprised. Tamburlaine serenades her with poetry but, when she eventually dies, rages against the dying of the light. The fact that Zenocrate specifically asked him to be 'patient' (2.4.67) and to contain his 'fury' (2.4.68) is forgotten. It is as if he regards rage as the only kind of emotional response which is not effeminate. Zenocrate is being worshipped and despised at the same time, in death as in life. Despite her pleas for an end to bloodshed, Tamburlaine buries her with rivers of blood. He destroys the town in which she died. It becomes a sight both of his power and powerlessness:

> This cursed town will I consume with fire,
> Because this place bereft me of my love.
> The houses, burnt, will look as if they mourn'd;
> And here will I set up her stature,
> And march about it with my mourning camp,
> Drooping and pining for Zenocrate. (2.4.137–42)

It is hardly a fit memorial for somebody who lamented the carnage that took place during the sack of Damascus. The statue is accompanied by a plaque which records, or registers, 'all her virtues and perfections' (3.2.23). It does not tell her story of the siege of Damascus. Her body is embalmed and wrapped in a sheet of gold so that it can be paraded near the battlefields. Her picture is hung up outside Tamburlaine's tent to give him an added military advantage, in much the same way as Sir Humphrey Gilbert lined up heads outside his own tent:

> Thou shalt be set upon my royal tent;
> And when I meet an army in the field,
> Those looks will shed such influence in my camp
> As if Bellona, goddess of the war,

> Threw naked swords and sulphur-balls of fire
> Upon the heads of all our enemies. (3.2.37–42)

Just as he displayed her to Theridamas as part of the play to get
him to change sides, so he now displays her picture to his troops to
encourage them to fight harder.

Zenocrate's death prompts Tamburlaine to make long speeches
to his sons glorifying the very arts of war which had caused her so
much distress:

> View me, thy father, that hath conquer'd kings,
> And with his host march'd round about the earth,
> Quite void of scars and clear from any wound,
> That by the wars lost not a dram of blood,
> And see him lance his flesh to teach you all.
> A wound is nothing, be it ne'er so deep;
> Blood is the god of war's rich livery. (3.2.110–16)

He uses his own body to construct another sight of power. His
younger sons respond enthusiastically to such lessons on military
discipline. Calyphas finds the sight, or view, of his father letting his
own blood a 'pitiful' (3.2.130) rather than a powerful one.

Calyphas, like Mycetes, has no stomach for fighting. He also
considers battles to be too much of a lottery and so is prepared to
let others run the risks. Despite the entreaties and warnings of his
younger brothers, he remains in his tent playing cards with his
servant. Tamburlaine waited until he had an audience before
taking Mycetes's crown. He is equally conscious of the need to
stage a sight of power when he kills Calyphas. He drags his son out
of the tent and makes him stand before both the armies. He
refuses to listen to pleas for clemency because that would be to
condone effeminacy. He kills his supposedly effeminate son as a
way of demonstrating his own masculinity. The rebel crushes the
rebellion of his eldest son. The defeated Turks, who form part of
the on-stage audience for this execution, are quick to condemn it.
The King of Jerusalem may be articulating the responses and
expectations of many spectators when he declares:

> Thy victories are grown so violent
> That shortly heaven, fill'd with the meteors

Of blood and fire thy tyrannies have made,
Will pour down blood and fire on thy head,
Whose scalding drops will pierce thy seething brains,
And with our bloods, revenge our bloods on thee. (4.1.138–43)

Expectations of divine intervention are, once again, set up only to be undermined. Calyphas's punishment does not end with his death. Tamburlaine orders some of his followers to:

> Ransack the tents and the pavilions
> Of these proud Turks, and take their concubines,
> Making them bury this effeminate brat;
> For not a common soldier shall defile
> His manly fingers with so faint a boy. (4.2.159–63)

The concubines are divided up amongst the common soldiers after they have buried Calyphas. Tamburlaine may upset the expectations of his enemies in Part One by being a courtly lover rather than a rapist. He nevertheless encourages others to commit rape.

The gods do not intervene to prevent Tamburlaine from passing both his crown and chariot to Amyras before dying a natural death. His enemies frequently represented him as an anarchic figure who inhabited a region that was either off their maps altogether, or else close to the margins of them. He ends the play by showing his remaining sons how his conquests have re-drawn large parts of the map of the world. He urges them to complete the task. Zenocrate's body is brought on-stage towards the end of the scene. It is there when Tamburlaine commands Amyras to 'scourge and control those slaves' (5.3.228) who pull the chariot.

The *Tamburlaine* plays appear to be permeated with misogyny. Zenocrate is put on display to impress Theridamas and thus to bring Tamburlaine closer to the Persian crown. This is perhaps why she needed to be 'flattered'. Her identity begins to disintegrate when her loyalties are divided between her father and her future husband. Tamburlaine refuses to spare the citizens of Damascus and only reluctantly grants a reprieve to the Soldan. He is afraid that he will become effeminate if he listens to Zenocrate's voice. The Virgins are speared to death and then displayed on the walls of the city at the same time as he is praising Zenocrate's purity and beauty. She catalogues the carnage of the siege and laments the 'bloody spectacle' of Zabina's mutilated body. Part One ends with a truce, not just to the fighting itself but also to anxieties about how women might undermine masculine strength. The truce does not last into Part Two. Tamburlaine wants to replace Zenocrate's influence over their children with his own. She asks him not to damage her after-life by responding rashly to her impending death. He burns a city to the ground and hangs up her picture outside his tent so that his soldiers will fight harder. He then kills the son who takes after his mother. The concubines bury the corpse and are then distributed among the common soldiers.

Simon Shepherd suggests in *Marlowe and the Politics of Elizabethan Theatre* (1986) that the plays may question misogynist attitudes by the very way in which they are reproduced. He argues, for instance, that the power relationships which are implicit in love poetry become explicit, and therefore more open to question, when placed in a dramatic context. Spectators can see that Zenocrate is either silent or absent when Tamburlaine praises her beauty. His control of the discourse is highlighted by his control of the physical space of the stage. It is an argument that works particularly well as far as the siege of Damascus is concerned. There may be times when misogyny is revealed rather than being merely reproduced and yet the plays as a whole do not explore alternatives to it. Zenocrate's voice is either stifled by Tamburlaine's poetic flattery, or else ignored. Zabina goes mad and kills herself. Although not dealt with for reasons of space, Olympia also commits a form of suicide in Part Two. The Virgins of Damascus are killed. The options available for women are both limited and negative. The treatment of Calyphas suggests that the man's part also has severe limitations imposed upon it.

The *Tamburlaine* plays have acquired a reputation for being difficult and inaccessible. This may have something to do with the fact that they are not performed regularly and so the criticism on them is not always as attuned as it might be to the different ways in which particular themes can be treated. It has tended, in other words, to underestimate the openness of the texts. There is, nevertheless, a growing awareness of the need to concentrate attention on the questions that are posed instead of providing dogmatic answers to them. The plays continually interrogate the assumptions and expectations of their spectators on such issues as colonisation, costume, rebellion, kingship, divine intervention and military etiquette. They raise some questions about the performance of the woman's part even though many dominant assumptions appear to be retained.

5
The Jew of Malta

5.1 The Monologue of Power

Malta is governed by the Knights Hospitallers of Saint John of Jerusalem, a religious order which was formed in accordance with the crusading ideals of chivalry. The Knights established themselves in Malta in 1522, after they had been driven out of Rhodes by the Turks. Their members were recruited from the aristocracies of Europe. They were attacked again by the Turks in 1565 but managed, against all the odds, to hold Malta during a four-month siege. Their leader, Jean Parisot de la Valette, became the hero of Christendom. *The Jew of Malta* represents a Turkish siege of Malta, although it does not deal directly with the events of what quickly became known as the Great Siege of 1565. Most Elizabethan spectators would nevertheless have been familiar with at least the outlines of stories about this famous victory. As suggested, Marlowe's plays take great delight in challenging assumptions and expectations. His spectators are therefore presented with a very different story about Malta and its struggles with the Turks.

Marlowe's Knights make solemn and ceremonious entrances and exits. Their power, like that of Queen Elizabeth, is displayed through processions or passages. Their leader, Ferneze, is a man of few words who is more accustomed to command than obey. He is nevertheless on the defensive since Calymath and the Turks hold the military advantage. All he can do is try to buy some precious time before he is forced to play an overdue tribute. He obtains a month's grace which, under the circumstances, represents a good bargain for Christendom.

The Turks depart taking him at his word. Their generosity and trust provide a striking contrast to hostile propaganda images of them. Martin Luther's *On War Against the Turk* (1529) sets the tone by representing them as the scourges of Christendom who were in league with Lucifer. Archery practice in Elizabethan England, which some moralists declared was in decline because of the rise of the public theatres, was known as 'shooting at the Turk'. Turks also provided a butt for nationalistic prejudices in popular drama. Mummers' plays show Saint George triumphing over the Turkish Knight. It was commonplace to describe villains as 'turning Turk' when they revealed their true intentions. The Politic Bankrupt in Dekker's *The Seven Deadly Sins of London* (1606) pretends to be a Protestant and 'deals justly with all men till he sees his time, but in the end he turns Turk' (p.17). He is in fact Barabbas Bankruptisme, a rich Jew of London. John Stubbes's *The Discoverie of a Gaping Gulf* declares that the French have turned Turk as a result of making peace with Turkey in 1536. The *Tamburlaine* plays do not challenge these views of the Turks. This seems true of the representation of Bajazeth in Part One although Callapine in Part Two can be seen, albeit momentarily, in a more positive light. *The Jew of Malta* nevertheless self-consciously refuses to demonise the Turkish warriors. It therefore has more in common with the views that lay behind attempts to open up trading and diplomatic ties with Turkey. Elizabeth's correspondence with the Sultan in 1579, the same year that Stubbes took it upon himself to criticise Turkish tyranny, helped to prepare the way for the foundation of the Levant Company the following year. There were also attempts during the final decades of the sixteenth century to persuade the Turks to play a more active part in attacking Spanish ships in the Western Mediterranean. Sir Antony Sherley's attempts to build alliances against the Turks threatened such initiatives.

The Jew of Malta shows the Turks to be generous, if somewhat too trusting. Ferneze's generosity and trustworthiness are called into question when he orders the Jews of Malta to be brought into his presence. It is clear that he made his plans to levy the tribute before the meeting with the Turks. It rapidly becomes apparent that he has thought of a way of raising the money in a matter of minutes rather than weeks. The Jews are requested to make a contribution to the general good. Barabas's heckling reveals that this request is in fact an order. Ferneze drops his diplomatic mask: 'For, to be short, amongst you't must be had' (1.2.57). Is there any room, however small, for dialogue and debate? No, because Ferneze has had 'the articles of our decrees' (1.2.68) written out before he meets both the Jews and the Turks. These 'articles' are framed in such a way as to anticipate all objections to them. They represent the monologue of power. All of Barabas's property is eventually confiscated because he makes the mistake of challenging them. Ferneze crushes any further dispute:

> No, Jew, we take particularly thine
> To save the ruin of a multitude.
> And better one want for a common good,
> Than many perish for a private man. (1.2.95–8)

The Christian Governor ironically borrows the words that were used by the Jewish High Priest to justify the crucifixion of Christ. Categories are beginning to become dangerously unstable: Turks appear to be more trustworthy than Christians and Christians begin to sound like Jews.

Ferneze is given an opportunity to break his promise to the Turks with the arrival of Martin Del Bosco, the Spanish Vice-Admiral, who has come to sell a cargo of 'Grecians, Turks, and Afric Moors' (2.2.9) which has been captured from a Turkish galley. Ferneze's motives may be mercenary and opportunistic, but he wraps them in crusading rhetoric:

> Proud-daring Calymath, instead of gold,
> We'll send thee bullets wrapt in smoke and fire.
> Claim tribute where thou wilt, we are resolv'd;
> Honour is bought with blood, and not with gold. (2.2.54–7)

Ferneze's honour has nevertheless been bought with both Jewish gold and the prospect of a share in the profits from the slave market.

A Turkish Knight comes to demand that the tribute is paid. He is concerned with gold rather than honour:

> *Ferneze*: What wind drives you thus into Malta road?
> *Basso:*   The wind that bloweth all the world besides,
>   Desire of gold.   (3.5.3–5)

The Turks are refreshingly honest about their motives. Ferneze declares that he will pay nothing to 'heathens' (3.5.12). He believes, like Sigismund in the second part of *Tamburlaine the Great*, that he is under no obligation to honour promises to unbelievers. He seeks to rally the Knights of Saint John with some more fighting talk after the Basso has made a dignified exit:

> And let's provide to welcome Calymath.
> Close your portcullis, charge your basilisks,
> And as you profitably take up arms,
> So now courageously encounter them; . . . (3.5.30–3)

Just as honour is associated with buying and selling, so war is · linked with profit.

Ferneze is only able to discover the true extent of Barabas's crimes with the help of Bellamira and Pilia-Borza, grotesque characters from the underworld who are also blown into his presence by a desire for gold. He immediately gives orders for Barabas to be tortured: 'Make fires, heat irons, let the rack be fetched' (5.1.23). One of the Knights has to remind him that he ought to wait and see if there is a chance of a voluntary confession before resorting to torture. He uncharacteristically relents and has Barabas marched off to prison. The news arrives moments later that Barabas has died in prison. Del Bosco finds 'This sudden death of his is very strange' (5.1.51). Spectators may share his surprise. Ferneze merely sees it all as the will of Heaven. He orders the outcast to be literally cast out:

> For the Jew's body, throw that o'er the walls,
> To be a prey for vultures and wild beasts. (5.1.55–6)

Ferneze may have been deprived of the spectacle of Barabas's suffering but, in keeping with the official script for the theatre of

Hell, he tries to make sure that punishment continues even after death. He consigns Barabas's body to that marginal area beyond the walls of the city. This can, in performance, become the space that is occupied by the spectators themselves. Barabas has not in fact been disposed of by divine intervention. He is only shamming death. He rises again from the dead and does not need three days to do so. He falls into the hands of Calymath and the Turkish army, who are laying siege to the island in order to claim their tribute. He leads a party of Turks through the 'common channels' (5.1.86), or sewers, to make a successful surprise attack. It is a triumphant return of the repressed. The outcasts move from the margins to the centre through the very channels which the Christians use to cast out all traces of the grotesque body. Calymath keeps his promise to Barabas by making him Governor of the island. He orders the aristocratic Christian Knights to kneel before him and suggests that Ferneze has made a tactical blunder by placing too much faith in the power of Christian Spain. Del Bosco appears to have broken his promise to provide Spanish protection for the island. Ferneze refuses to get involved in this ritual humiliation: 'What should I say? We are captives, and must yield' (5.2.6). He is less guarded in his reactions to Barabas's appointment as Governor and clings to the belief that, ultimately, there will be some form of divine intervention to preserve his own authority.

Barabas is given clear indications of Ferneze's continuing hostility. He nevertheless decides to make a friend of his enemy. It is an error of judgement which runs counter to Machiavelli's specific advice on how to treat enemies. Barabas also ignores Machiavelli's more general advice on statecraft when he is so open with Ferneze about the details of the plot against the Turks. Ferneze is, by contrast, much more cautious and guarded. Initially, he asks questions instead of making revealing statements. A bargain is struck whereby Barabas agrees to rid Malta of the Turks in exchange for the 'Great sums of money' (5.2.89), which Ferneze guarantees to raise. Ferneze will continue to be Governor when the operation has been completed. The way in which Barabas needs to boast about his own cunning reveals his lack of it.

Barabas compounds his original errors by allowing Ferneze to play an important part in the counter-attack against the Turks. This means that he needs to reveal even more of his plan:

Now as for Calymath and his consorts,
Here have I made a dainty gallery,
The floor whereof, this cable being cut,
Doth fall asunder, so that it doth sink
Into a deep pit past recovery.
Here, hold that knife; and when thou seest he comes,
And with his bassoes shall be blithely set,
A warning-piece shall be shot off from the tower,
To give the knowledge when to cut the cord,
And fire the house. Say, will not this be brave? (5.5.34-42)

Ferneze responds very briefly: 'O, excellent!' (5.5.44). He takes care to conceal his intentions.

Barabas dominates the stage not just because his speeches fill almost all of its empty spaces, but also because the plot against the Turks demands that he has to rebuild parts of it. The stage directions give an indication of the frenzied way in which he sets about these alterations: '*Enter* Barabas *with a hammer above, very busy, and* Carpenters' (5.5). His domination of the stage is underlined by the way in which his thoughts become the cues for the other actors. He dismisses the carpenters (to their deaths) after he has made sure that the stage machinery is working correctly. He then indicates that he is still waiting for Calymath to accept the invitation. A messenger enters with an acceptance. He wonders whether Ferneze has collected the money. Ferneze immediately enters with the money and is then treated to the gloating description of the 'dainty gallery'. The conflict between Barabas and Ferneze is given specifically theatrical dimensions. Barabas's overflowing rhetoric, reconstruction of the stage and ability to cue entrances at will signify his power. It is a power which resembles that of the dramatist. Barabas and Ferneze are rival playwrights who compete with each other for the authorship of the play in general and its final scene in particular.

Ferneze's script calls for Barabas's public execution. Thanks to his careful rehearsal of some complicated stage business, it is Barabas rather than Calymath who falls through the trapdoor in the gallery into the cauldron below. The Knights of Saint John, aided by Del Bosco, have recaptured the stage and therefore their power. They initially occupy the gallery which, as will be seen, is where Lucifer and his followers position themselves for Faustus's execution. Most of them then probably descend to the stage, or scaffold, itself. Ferneze, who was forced to kneel before the Turks, is now able to command them to form an audience for the spectacle of Barabas's death: 'See his end first' (5.5.71). Barabas appeals unsuccessfully to this on-stage audience: 'Governor, why stand you all so pitiless?' (5.5.73). Ferneze's orthodox script allows no pity for the condemned man and insists that there should be a spectacle of suffering in a theatre of Hell. Barabas still tries to subvert the spectacle by refusing to beg for forgiveness in his dying speech. His earlier control of the stage was characterised by the speed of events: '*Enter* Barabas . . . *very busy*'. Now the tempo has changed: there is time for an audience to be grouped self-consciously on the stage. Ferneze is a dramatist who writes scenes in which groupings on stage are designed to provide sights of his power. The agony of Barabas's death is prolonged by the fact that the cauldron takes some time to heat up. The condemned man has an opportunity to confess his crimes, but he continues to curse his executioners. He throws their script, with its acknowledgement of divine intervention and retribution, back at them by blaming only his bad luck, or fortune, for his downfall:

> And had I but escap'd this stratagem,
> I would have brought confusion on you all,
> Damn'd Christians, dogs, and Turkish infidels! (5.5.86–8)

It is only the increasing 'extremity of heat' (5.5.89) that stops his mouth and therefore puts a stop to this subversion of the part that Ferneze has written for him.

Ferneze supplies an orthodox conclusion to the spectacle of Barabas's suffering:

> So march away; and let due praise be given,
> Neither to Fate nor Fortune, but to Heaven. (5.5.125–6)

The Knights slowly and deliberately process off-stage. Some Elizabethan spectators may well have marched away from the theatre accepting such a resolution. Almost infinite room is nevertheless provided for spectators to reject this official script. There is a problem about the way in which Ferneze so openly controls the on-stage spectators. The Turks are, quite literally, a captive audience. Perhaps he wishes to enslave the paying customers as well. The mention of money complicates matters even more. Ferneze pockets the money extorted from the Jews at the beginning of the play. He probably takes a substantial cut from the profits of the slave market. It seems highly likely that he will keep the bag containing the 'hundred thousand pounds' (5.5.21) which he raised to pay Barabas for changing sides. Perhaps he is still carrying it when he delivers the orthodox resolution. He will almost certainly get a good ransom for Calymath. His final couplet is a terse monologue of power which may nevertheless provoke, rather than suppress, dialogue and debate.

Marlowe is often accused of writing plays in which the central character eclipses all others. This ignores the fact that the plays dramatise struggles for centrality. It is dangerous to underestimate the importance of Ferneze – for Barabas, of course, it is fatal to do so. He is certainly a man of few words and these happen to be remarkably prosaic ones. His speeches are usually cautious and guarded, although they are sometimes filled with the slightly loftier cadences of the propaganda tract. Rhetorically, he represents a classical body which is enclosed and sealed off. His words do not engulf the stage. They do not spill over, either through asides or more direct forms of address, to embrace the spectators. Like Walsingham, he is loath to lay himself open to anybody. He retains rather than reveals his thoughts. Barabas ends up violating some of Machiavelli's fundamental principles of statecraft. Ferneze, by contrast, provides an object lesson in how to act upon them by appearing not to do so.

5.2 The Many Faces of Machiavelli

The play opens with a Prologue delivered by Machevill, the ghost of Machiavelli. He clearly identifies Barabas as one of his disciples:

> I come not, I,
> To read a lecture here in Britanie,
> But to present the tragedy of a Jew,
> Who smiles to see how full his bags are cramm'd;
> Which money was not got without my means.

> I crave but this: grace him as he deserves,
> And let him not be entertain'd the worse
> Because he favours me. (28–35)

His style is provocative. He does not need to deliver a 'lecture' in Britain because his ideas are already too well-known to the spectators. His manner is nevertheless also secretive. He reveals Barabas's discipleship, but conceals the identities of his other followers. He provides some clues, but no names, earlier on in the Prologue:

> To some perhaps my name is odious,
> But such as love me guard me from their tongues . . . (5–6)

His tongue guards the play's secret that Ferneze employs a subversive creed to control subversion.

The representation of Machevill is similar to Protestant propaganda images that were circulated during the French religious wars by Innocent Gentillet and others. Both versions cast Machiavelli as a melodramatic villain. The Machevill/Make-Evil of the Prologue is associated with poison, atheism, murder and the doctrine of might is right. The earlier chapters of Machiavelli's *The Prince*, which was probably completed towards the end of 1513, can appear to be very tame when set alongside such catalogues of vice. There are nevertheless chapters later on which suggest why Machiavelli was to acquire such a sinister reputation. He argues that truth can, and on occasions must, be subordinated to necessity:

> a prudent ruler cannot, and should not, honour his word when it places him at a disadvantage and when the reasons for which he made his promise no longer exist. If all men were good, this precept would not be good; but because men are wretched creatures who would not keep their word to you, you need not keep your word to them. (1971 Penguin edition, pp. 99–100)

Machiavelli adds that a ruler may nevertheless find it to his 'advantage' to 'appear' to be truthful. This becomes part of a wider argument about relationships between appearances and realities.

Real generosity is too expensive, whereas the appearance of generosity costs nothing and may well purchase everything.

The content is controversial and yet it is not accompanied by a polemical, provocative style. Although Marlowe's Machevill is cautious about names, his manner and mannerisms are overstated and aggressive. He flaunts himself and taunts the spectators. Machiavelli's manner, by contrast, is often understated, Indeed, his guarded, heavily qualified style appears to complement and reinforce his message that it is dangerous for true intentions to be disclosed. Wayne A. Rebhorn suggests in *Foxes and Lions: Machiavelli's Confidence Men* (1988) that Machiavelli 'forces his readers to adopt a particularly active role in deciphering his texts' (p. 209). Rebhorn emphasises the element of force and so is able to identify the ways in which Machiavelli controls his readers, while appearing to encourage their activity. Marlowe's Machevill seeks to control the audience in more obvious and direct ways.

The difficulties involved in deciphering Machiavelli's meanings helped to create and sustain the propaganda images. His silences often cried out to be articulated, just as some of his qualifications begged to be ignored. He states that men will act wickedly unless they are compelled by necessity to be good. The first part of this proposition does not appear to depart from Christian teachings about original sin, although the second part seems to deny a doctrine which also emphasises love. The fact that Machiavelli took care not to spell out precisely how far he was departing from Christianity allowed the propagandists to fashion an image of him as an atheist. Stubbes's *The Discoverie of a Gaping Gulf* accuses members of the French court of being both Machiavellian atheists and cruel Turks:

> This is that most Christian court where Machiavelli is their New Testament and atheism is their religion, yea, whose whole policy and government seems to set the Turkish tyranny as a pattern, and they draw as near to it as their ancient laws will any ways suffer in so small time. (p. 76)

Atheism is also the religion of Marlowe's Machevill:

> I count religion but a childish toy,
> And hold there is no sin but ignorance. (14–15)

Machiavelli's own position is more complicated. He certainly appears to be relatively uninterested in doctrinal issues and this helped to sustain the belief that he was an atheist. He is nevertheless concerned with religion as a social institution. His *Discourses*, which remained unfinished at his death (in 1527), reveal a fascination with the ways in which the ferocity of certain Pagan religions played a part in maintaining both military and social discipline. His critique of Catholicism in *The Prince* is not so much that it is a 'childish toy', but, rather, that it is hindering rather than helping Italian unification. He does not therefore dismiss religious institutions out of hand, but seeks to show how they need to become more effective political instruments.

It is difficult to know how many Elizabethans had actually read Machiavelli as opposed to reading about him in hostile tracts. Some of his works were banned from being published in English. The suggestion that well-educated members of the society would nevertheless have had access to some version of the texts themselves, as well as to the propaganda that was fashioned out of them, is supported by the representation of Machiavellianism in *The Jew of Malta*. Ferneze is close to the spirit of Machiavelli's own writings, whereas Machevill comes out of the popular propaganda that became associated with these writings. Ferneze breaks his word to both Calymath and Barabas in keeping with the rules of conduct recommended in *The Prince*. He also follows Machiavelli's related advice on how to treat enemies who want to become friends. His guarded style is close to Machiavelli's own and far removed from the flamboyance of both Machevill and Barabas.

Machiavelli is a profoundly contradictory writer. *Discourses* recommends the sinews of discipline as a cure for what is seen as an effeminate body politic. Tamburlaine and, as will be seen, Mortimer in *Edward II* offer versions of this argument. The methods and institutions of discipline are also strongly recommended in *The Art of War*, which was first translated into English in 1560. Such inherently conservative messages are nevertheless in danger of being subverted by the way in which Machiavelli's theories also propose a chaotic dislocation between outward signs, or shows, and inward meanings. He offers, at one and the same time, the stability of discipline and the instabilities associated with theatrical appearances and representations. This contradiction can be explored in relation to his definition of *virtú*. Its meanings are characteristically difficult to decipher. The nearest equivalent in English is not virtue but virility, or perhaps vigour. *Virtú* does not just encompass an abstract list of what are taken to be manly virtues. It also emphasises the ability to put the abstract into practice. Discipline may be a key part of *virtú* and yet theatrical cunning is often essential to make it prevail. It requires a combination of action and acting. Tamburlaine clearly possesses *virtú*, as do characters from the stage-play world such as Ralegh and Walsingham. The Babington conspirators had some of the theatrical talents admired by Machiavelli and yet they proved that they were not men of action.

It is tempting to consider the possibility that *The Jew of Malta* dramatises some of the conflicts within Machiavelli's own writings. There is, after all, a struggle for power between a ruler who uses Machiavelli's ideas to maintain traditional forms of social discipline and a highly theatrical alien stranger who exploits them for subversive purposes. It is the conservative Machiavellian who is allowed to have a very precarious victory. The problem with such an interpretation is that it tends to transform *The Jew of Malta* into a self-conscious play of ideas, which could only have been understood by a coterie of spectators who possessed a detailed knowledge of Machiavelli. It was, however, a play which enjoyed success in the public theatres.

It may, therefore, make more sense to see the play as being about propaganda in general rather than confining it to specific debates about Machiavelli. Machevill, the Italianate atheist, and Barabas, the villainous Jew, are examples of how society constructs its other through both formal and informal propaganda. The centre defines and perpetuates itself by creating a demonology inhabited by caricatures of the outcast or alien stranger. *The Jew of Malta* confronts Elizabethan spectators with their own representations of this demonised other. The confrontation is achieved theatrically, as it is in the *Tamburlaine* plays, by allowing marginalised characters to hold the centre of the stage. Machevill's Prologue is followed by the long scene set in Barabas's counting house. Such a movement from the margins to the centre may please as well as provoke spectators. The marginal figure has often been an object of suppressed desire as well as open disgust. The representation of Machiavellianism is just one of the ways in which the play questions the categories of the propagandist. Machiavellianism is the creed of a marginalised character, who is provocatively brought to the centre of the stage. It then turns out also to be the creed of the ruler himself, who is responsible for demonising Barabas. So categories become confused: the central resembles the marginal, the classical body is similar to the grotesque body and the ruler employs a subversive creed to control subversion. The play's main concern may not be to dramatise specific conflicts in and around Machiavelli's writings, but to reveal some of the contradictions inherent in the way in which society seeks both to define and police its margins.

5.3 The Jewish Grotesque

The watchmen of Enfield were convinced that they were supposed to apprehend somebody with 'a hooked nose' when the Babington conspirators were on the run in 1586. They appeared to believe that it was Jews rather than Catholics who had threatened to subvert Church and State. Their confusion was understandable since both Jews and Catholics were regarded as alien strangers. Jews had been officially expelled from England in 1290, although small communities still existed in the Elizabethan period. They were expected to wear a yellow cross to signal their status as aliens, just as beggars and others were forced to wear badges to identify their marginal status. Jews in fact usually purchased their continued existence through an outward show, or badge, of Christianity. The watchmen had therefore set themselves a difficult, but not absolutely impossible, task.

Perhaps they had more success in 1594 as this was the year when Jews temporarily replaced Catholics and advanced Puritans as the leading public enemies. This was a result of the trial and public execution of Roderigo Lopez, an elderly Portuguese Jew who became the Queen's personal physician in 1586. A token profession of Christianity allowed him to achieve professional recognition and status. It also meant that he was trusted to play a part in the Machiavellian world of the Elizabethan secret service. He was initially involved in supporting groups which sought to destabilise Spain, although he then appears to have had dealings aimed at securing peace with Spain. He thus antagonised the Earl of Essex, who was using hostility to Spain as one of his platforms, or stages, for displaying affection for the Queen. Essex, aided by Anthony Bacon, successfully fashioned Lopez into a Judas who had imagined poisoning the Queen. Lopez was tried at the Guildhall in February and executed at Tyburn in June. His declaration on the scaffold that he loved the Queen as much as he loved Christ was laughed down by the spectators. His alleged accomplices were also executed. One of them, Manuel Tinoco, emulated John Savage by putting up a good struggle on the scaffold. He managed to stand up after he was cut down from the gallows and had a bout with the executioner. He eventually had to be held down to have his 'privities' cut off. Although this particular incident appears to have turned the spectators against the spectacle, the Lopez affair in general confirmed a whole demonology.

The Jew of Malta, which was probably first performed in 1589, was revived in February 1594 and went through fifteen performances. This represents a commercial success, given the extended repertory system adopted by Elizabethan theatrical companies. It may be that the play, when watched against the background of mounting social hysteria, became for many spectators an unproblematic endorsement of Elizabethan propaganda. Perhaps they acknowledged that Barabas put up a good fight on the scaffold, but still marched away applauding his death. Perhaps, by contrast, they came to understand why their society needed scapegoats and how it set about constructing them. Both responses are possible since the play confirms as well as denies popular prejudices against Jews and other demonised groups.

Barabas was played on the Elizabethan stage in a deliberately confrontational manner. Edward Alleyn wore a long gabardine coat and a red wig. He also put on an outrageous hooked nose. Barabas's caricature appearance confirms the propagandist's categories of the central and the marginal, the classical and the grotesque. These categories are, however, also confused. Barabas wears the badges of a marginal character, yet he takes the centre of the stage. His counting house is at the centre of the commercial world. Merchants come and go at his bidding. He appears to control the elements themselves. Gold pours in from almost every corner of the known world. He is, at one and the same time, a marginalised figure and a master of the economic universe. His power and centrality are reinforced by his rhetoric. Ferneze's speeches are short, prosaic and unmemorable. Barabas, particularly

in the first two acts, is given some of Marlowe's most memorable
lines:

> This is the ware wherein consists my wealth;
> And thus, methinks, should men of judgement frame
> Their means of traffic from the vulgar trade,
> And as their wealth increaseth, so inclose
> Infinite riches in a little room. (1.1.32–6)

His rhetoric is infinitely richer than that of the other characters
who share the confined space of the stage with him.

Barabas's theatrical power is also emphasised by the way in
which only he is able to transcend the confinements of the stage by
cultivating a privileged relationship with the audience. As noted,
Ferneze's speeches and decrees are a monologue of power.
Barabas nevertheless attempts to interrupt their flow with questions and asides:

Officer: 'First, the tribute-money of the Turks shall all be levied
            amongst the Jews, and each of them to pay one-half of
            his estate'.
Barabas: How! Half his estate? I hope you mean not mine.
Ferneze: Read on.   (1.2.69–72)

Barabas fails to establish a dialogue with Ferneze, although is
more successful in reaching out to the audience. His asides to the
spectators may have provoked some hostile responses in 1594, but
at least they could not be accused of closing down debate.

Ferneze's characteristically curt 'Read on' indicates his reluc-
tance to depart from a written script. Barabas, by contrast, thrives
upon the excitement and risks of the improvised script. He kneels
down and curses the Christians, after they have processed slowly
off the stage. His on-stage audience consists of three other Jews.
He puts on a powerful performance both for them and the theatre
audience. He curses, boasts and then begins to mourn the loss of
his wealth. Perhaps both audiences are moved. Barabas then
quickly gets to his feet as soon as the Jews depart and stands
outside his own performance to reveal it as performance:

> See the simplicity of these base slaves,
> Who, for the villians have no wit themselves,

Think me to be a senseless lump of clay,
That will with every water wash to dirt!
No, Barabas is born to better chance,
And fram'd of finer mould than common men,
That measure naught but by the present time. (1.2.212–18)

The tone of the address is confrontational. Any spectators who found themselves sympathising with him are immediately branded, along with the three Jews, as being 'base slaves'. Like Tamburlaine, he rebels against linguistic badges. Marlowe's plays do not allow the meaning of terms such as 'base slave' and 'thief' to remain uncontested. Barabas's costume may signify his status as an alien stranger and yet he confidently asserts that he is 'fram'd of finer mould than common men'. He is able to back this up by revealing that he had anticipated trouble and so had hidden some of his money. This indicates that he was staging a performance for Ferneze as well as one for the three Jews. He confronts the spectators and yet, unlike Ferneze, also needs to share his secrets with them.

Barabas's ability both to perform and stand outside his own performance means that he has some similarities with the disruptive figure of Vice in earlier plays. Yet he is a development of Vice as he is given more specific motivation and allowed to cause disruption on a larger scale. He also has a poetic power that was usually denied to Vice. Both characters are accomplished improvisers, although in Marlowe's text improvisation acquires a set of specifically political associations through its links with Machiavellianism. Barabas also has some similarities with Jewish villains such as Herod and Judas from the Passion plays, although once again he transcends their limitations.

Barabas is forced to improvise another play within the play to retrieve the hidden money because Ferneze has ordered his house to be converted into a nunnery. This was suggested by one of the Knights and immediately sanctioned without further dialogue: 'It shall be so' (1.2.130). Barabas persuades his daughter, Abigail, to ask to join the nunnery. She interrupts the procession of nuns and monks that is on its way to the house. As already suggested, the power of the Knights is conveyed visually through the solemnity of their ceremonial processions on and off the stage. This is also true as far as the power of the Church is concerned. Although the stage directions themselves are not very helpful, there is a lot of other evidence to suggest that a religious procession would have been accompanied by music and chants on the Elizabethan stage. This happens in *Doctor Faustus*. Both plays allow actors to perform the parts of priests.

Barabas is initially content to play the part of a spectator, which may help to cement his relationship with the theatre audience. He then becomes an actor in his own drama, playing the part of a grotesque Jew at the same time as he provides Abigail with whispered instructions about the precise location of the money:

> *Barabas:* Child of perdition, and thy father's shame!
> What wilt thou do among these hateful fiends?
> I charge thee on my blessing that thou leave
> These devils and their damned heresy.
> *Abigail:* Father, give me —
> *Barabas:*   Nay, back, Abigail —
> And think upon the jewels and the gold;
> The board is marked thus that covers it.
> Away, accursed, from thy father's sight! (1.2.339–46)

The spectators are placed in an ambiguous position since Barabas is an alien stranger who, nevertheless, voices acceptable anti-Catholic prejudices. He is the bearer of prejudice as well as the victim of it. Spectators are also confronted with the more general problem of how to respond to a self-consciously grotesque character who speaks the best lines and stages the most entertaining performances.

5.4 Making a Reasonable Market

Abigail returns the gold, which Barabas hugs to himself. His demonstrative gestures contrast with Ferneze's more guarded stage presence. He is now able to resume his commercial activities and so makes his way to the slave market. The Knights have just processed off-stage. They are followed on to it by 'Officers *with* Ithamore *and other* Slaves' (2.3). Ferneze's honourable reasons for allowing the market to take place are questioned by the rapid juxtaposition of these two processions. The classical bodies exit and the grotesque bodies enter. The slaves may be despised and yet they provide valuable financial support for the Knights. Jews may be despised and yet they also provide this essential support. Each slave wears a badge in the form of a 'price written on his back' (2.3.3). The citizens of Malta are blown in to search for bargains. It is an appropriate setting for related forms of commodity broking and exchange. Ferneze's son, Lodowick, affects to buy a diamond from Barabas, although it is clear to both of them that they are really discussing the purchase of a jewel called Abigail. Mathias affects to borrow a book from Barabas, although it is clear to both of them that they are really discussing the permanent loan of Abigail. The young men think that they are being very clever in talking this coded language, but Barabas's asides to the audience reveal that they are merely being cast to perform in another of his improvised plays within the play.

Barabas needs somebody to help him stage his theatre of misrule and so casts an expert eye over the human meat rack to find a likely apprentice. He makes a good bargain and yet is not alone in this. Mathias and his mother, Katharine, scrutinise the merchandise with equal care. Barabas acts out a caricature version of Jewish avarice, particularly in the counting house and the nunnery garden scenes. He confirms rather than denies popular prejudices. Yet the categories that are taken as read are confused by the way in which the Christians at the centre act in much the same way as do the Jews who have been constructed as marginal. Katharine treats Barabas with contempt: 'Converse not with him; he is cast off from heaven' (2.3.156). She is nevertheless also casting about for bargains. Both Barabas and Katharine, together with Del Bosco and Ferneze, make what the First Officer calls 'a reasonable market' (2.3.160). The Christian traders are nevertheless allowed to be more equal than others in the market place.

The officers march off with those slaves who have not fetched their price. Barabas, the subversive playwright, is now in control of the stage. He begins his play by offering his new slave, Ithamore, a version of his own wicked life and times:

> As for myself, I walk abroad a-nights,
> And kill sick people groaning under walls;
> Sometimes I go about and poison wells;
> And now and then, to cherish Christian thieves,
> I am content to lose some of my crowns,

That I may, walking in my gallery,
See 'em go pinion'd along by my door. (2.3.172–8)

He self-consciously represents himself as a character who has been 'cast off from heaven'. Comedy is also achieved through the clash between a matter of fact language ('As for myself', 'Sometimes I go about', 'And now and then') and the outrageous nature of the alleged crimes. Barabas goes on to reveal his employment of Machiavellian stratagems. His chronicle of evil inflates propaganda images and therefore may deflate them. It ends comically with an everyday question to Ithamore: 'But tell me now, how hast thou spent thy time?' (2.3.199)

The spectators now have the opportunity to see whether Ithamore, the Turkish slave, can outbid Barabas to become the wickedest man in the world. The winner will be decided by the amount of horrid laughter provoked:

Faith, master,
·In setting Christian villages on fire,
Chaining of eunuchs, binding galley-slaves.
One time I was an hostler in an inn,
And in the night time secretly would I steal
To travellers' chambers, and there cut their throats; . . .

(2.3.200–5)

Barabas probably retains his title. As noted, the Turkish soldiers are more chivalrous than the Christian Knights. The point is underlined by the appearance of Ithamore who, by contrast, conforms to the propaganda image of the Turk as the scourge of Christendom. The play offers two very different representations of Turks, which is a way of challenging the monologic authority of propaganda. It does not, however, use the same strategy to question the representation of Jews.

The competition between Barabas and Ithamore forms a Prologue to Barabas's revenge play, in much the same way as Machevill/Make-Evil provides a Prologue to Marlowe's own play. The play itself is based around improvised scenes designed to provoke a jealous rivalry between Lodowick and Mathias over Abigail. It reaches its climax after Ithamore delivers 'a challenge feign'd from Lodowick' (2.3.371) to Mathias. Barabas's revenge against Ferneze's written decrees is to improvise, but also to write out in part, a script that decrees the deaths of Lodowick and Mathias. As indicated earlier, the conflict between Ferneze and Barabas is given specifically theatrical dimensions. They are rival playwrights. Spectators can see this rivalry in terms of an opposition between the theatre of rule and the theatre of misrule. Yet, as so often in the play, there is an invitation to question neat polarities and stable categories. Barabas's revenge is the product of Ferneze's revenge. Barabas's written words may be deceitful and yet Ferneze's decrees are economical with the truth. Barabas's script calls for death and destruction. His letter killeth. Ferneze's script also calls for death in the form of Barabas's public execution. There are thus some important similarities between the theatre of rule and the theatre of misrule.

Barabas has already used Abigail to play two parts in his revenge plays. He cast her as an aspiring novice and then forced her to play a part in which she appeared to be the aspiring lover of Lodowick. He trades in everything and upon everyone. Abigail's loyalty does not provide an exception to his general rules, which are the rules of the slave market. Ferneze is not that different when he laments the fact that he is unable to trade upon Lodowick's death in his new crusade against the Turks. Abigail decides to withdraw from this world in which everyone has a price on their backs by returning, this time in good faith, to the nunnery:

> But I perceive there is no love on earth,
> Pity in Jews, nor piety in Turks. (3.3.47-8)

Her rejection of her Jewishness means that the caricature of the evil Jew is not challenged by more positive representations. The play goes on to suggest that religious institutions do not provide an escape from the ethics of the slave market. The friars prove themselves to be just as keen as everybody else to make a 'reasonable market' when they think that there is a chance of getting their hands on Barabas's worldly goods.

Abigail tries to write her own story. Instead of allowing herself to be the victim of Barabas's 'so neatly plotted, and so well perform'd' (3.3.2) scripts, she writes a letter to him urging him to repent the error of his ways. It is, nevertheless, her death warrant as Barabas improvises another play which will also end in death.

He gleefully poisons a pot of porridge and then orders Ithamore to place it by the 'dark entry' (3.4.78) used by the nuns to receive gifts from the outside world. Dark entries and sewers are revealed to be the weak points in the defences of the Church and State.

Marlowe stirs a lot of anti-Catholic ingredients into his own pot. The friars are represented as being sexually permissive and economically mercenary. They belong to the world of Elizabethan jestbooks, which in turn drew upon the traditions of medieval satire. *The Jew of Malta* certainly reproduces Protestant propaganda. Its anti-Spanish themes, associated with the way in which Del Bosco encourages the breaking of promises and then appears to break his own word, can also be seen as lending support to the propaganda of the 1580s. Spanish Vice-Admirals could not expect an enthusiastic reception in the Elizabethan theatres around the time of the Spanish Armada (1588). Yet *The Jew of Malta*, like the *Tamburlaine* plays, also exhibits the double movements that are so characteristic of Elizabethan drama. It offers the pleasures of the unfamiliar. It is set in Malta and represents characters who were not seen everyday in the streets of London. Yet it also appears to allow audiences to confirm familiar prejudices against such characters. The censor could hardly object. The play is nevertheless capable of producing shocks of recognition. Ferneze, like Queen Elizabeth, maintains power by suppressing dialogue. He stages processions as well as the spectacle of Barabas's suffering. The friars may resemble those in Elizabethan jestbooks and yet they can also be seen as vehicles for a wider critique of a mercenary Christianity.

As indicated, one of the functions of Machevill's Prologue is to bring the themes of the play closer to home by declaring that Elizabethan audiences require no lectures about Machiavelli. The play certainly contains an orthodox script which jests at friars, criticises the Spanish navy and demonises Jews. Yet this script can double back on itself to produce more topical and subversive meanings. Modern productions such as the 1987 Royal Shakespeare Company version like to dress the characters in carefully researched period costumes. Ferneze and his Knights wore flowing white tunics which were emblazoned with the Maltese cross. Elizabethan companies were not so fussy about the authenticity of their costumes. It is possible that, in Marlowe's time, these characters would have been dressed in recognisably Elizabethan costumes. They would therefore have been both unfamiliar and instantly recognisable.

Barabas's poisoned porridge works slowly and so Abigail's death is a lingering one. She has time to confess her part in the deaths of Lodowick amd Mathias to Friar Barnardine. She also hands him a written confession. She is treated as a commodity in death as in life. Friar Barnardine only regrets her death because she died a virgin and therefore remained free from a sexual market place in which some traders are more equal than others. She has nevertheless given him a valuable commodity in the form of information and, leaving her lying on the ground, he speeds off to market it. His actions are Machiavellian according to the definitions of the Prologue and yet, like Barabas, he breaks the golden rule by deciding not to act alone. He makes the mistake of involving Friar Jacomo in his plot to blackmail Barabas.

The friars are comically inept disciples of Machiavelli who are easy prey for the more accomplished Barabas. The victimisers are transformed into the victims. As Machiavelli himself puts it in *Discourses*, the little birds of prey are too busy with their own schemes to notice the shadow of the greater bird of prey who is going to destroy them. Barabas, characteristically informing the audience of his true intentions through an aside, affects an unlikely desire to convert to Christianity and invites the two friars to make rival bids for his worldly goods. Just as the Christians made a 'reasonable market' out of Del Bosco's galley slaves, so the two friars hope to make a 'reasonable market' out of Barabas's soul. Barabas successfully played the two lovers, Lodowick and Mathias, off against each other and now he improvises a broadly similar script for the two friars. His 'plot' is communicated directly to the audience:

What if I murder'd him ere Jacomo comes?
Now I have such a plot for both their lives,
As never Jew nor Christian knew the like: . . .(4.1.116–18)

Lodowick and Mathias kill each other. This new 'plot' involves Jacomo being framed for a murder which has been committed by Barabas and Ithamore. They prop up Barnardine's corpse and then take up their positions as a concealed on-stage audience.

Jacomo attacks the corpse thinking it is still alive and so is easily
persuaded that he is the real murderer. Just as Barabas the
playwright created the illusion that Abigail loved Lodowick, so his
more complicated stagecraft conveys the illusion that Jacomo
killed Barnardine. The spectators share the secrets of Barabas's
stagecraft and are therefore perhaps implicated in the original
crime and its cover-up.

5.5 The Christian Grotesque

Maltese justice accepts Barabas's theatrical illusion as reality.
Ferneze's theatre of rule is made to seem remarkably fallible.
Ithamore is a spectator when Jacomo performs to perfection the
part that Barabas has written for him:

> I never knew a man take his death so patiently as this friar. He
> was ready to leap off ere the halter was about his neck; and
> when the hangman had put on his hempen tippet, he made such
> haste to his prayers, as if he had another cure to serve.
>
> (4.2.21–4)

The execution is also watched by Pilia-Borza, who has instructions
from Bellamira to lure Ithamore to her house by giving him a love
letter. The shadow of the scaffold, like the public theatres
themselves, is revealed to be a market place for bawdy transactions and exchanges. This is not part of the official script for the
spectacle of suffering. Bellamira's letter is another of the play's
feigned challenges. She is a prostitute who claims to have fallen on
hard times when Malta is besieged by the Turks. Crusades may be
good for business as far as Ferneze is concerned, but they restrict
the commercial activities of some of his subjects. Bellamira
therefore plots with Pilia-Borza to steal Barabas's gold.

The spectators are asked to decide whether there is any real
difference between Bellamira's scheme and that already imple-
mented by Ferneze's decrees. Both she and Ferneze respond to
economic difficulties by scapegoating Barabas. Although she may
not have access to Ferneze's range of theological justifications,
their motives and actions are nevertheless remarkably similar. The

play's subversive script suggests affinities between the Christian Governor and the prostitute. It also allows her activities to be linked even more specifically with those of the Church. The friars make a clumsy attempt to blackmail Barabas with information obtained from Abigail's confession, whereas Bellamira is more successful at extorting money with menaces on the basis of Ithamore's confessions to her about his master. The play indicates correspondences between State, Church and brothel in Catholic Malta. Its double movement raises the question of whether this is also the case in Protestant England.

Bellamira and Pilia-Borza inhabit the criminal underworld. They are also nominally members of a Christian society and so claim the right to victimise Barabas. Bellamira is nevertheless represented as being a poorer version of Barabas. They both despise silver in favour of gold. They both take a professional pride in the way in which they appear to be at the centre of a commercial world:

> From Venice merchants, and from Padua
> Were wont to come rare-witted gentlemen,
> Scholars, I mean, learned and liberal; . . . (3.1.6–8)

The only difference is that the glories of Bellamira's counting house are all in the past. Her last refuge is to clutch at the popular prejudices that allow her to demonise the more successful merchant. It has become a familiar story.

As indicated, Elizabethan audiences were confronted by a self-consciously grotesque Barabas wearing a large false nose. They were also confronted by the grotesque body of Pilia-Borza. He has lost some of his fingers and so has to use his 'hooks' (3.1.19) in order to clamber up to steal from Barabas's counting house. He is, according to Barabas,

> . . . a shaggy totter'd staring slave,
> That when he speaks, draws out his grisly beard,
> And winds it twice or thrice about his ear;
> Whose face has been a grindstone for men's swords;
> His hands are hack'd, some fingers cut quite off,
> Who, when he speaks, grunts like a hog, . . . (4.3.6–11)

Pilia-Borza may be a soldier of fortune, who has had the misfortune to have both his face and hands hacked about while fighting in supposedly holy wars. He can therefore be seen as the grotesque reality that Ferneze's crusading rhetoric about war tries to conceal. He may, alternatively, be a braggart or counterfeit soldier. If so, then he has presumably been dismembered and disfigured in duels in the Maltese equivalents of Hog Lane. He certainly haunts the 'back lanes' (3.1.17) of Malta. The Christians claim that alien strangers like Turks and Jews are grotesque. This is challenged by allowing the most grotesque character in the play to exploit the Christian demonisation of Barabas for his own advantage.

Bellamira and Ithamore set about blackmailing Barabas, using Pilia-Borza as a go-between. The two blackmailers, one well past her prime and the other dressed in rags, nevertheless use a classical language of love in an attempt to conceal the mercenary realities of their relationship. Their declarations of love are, in more specifically theatrical terms, merely padding to fill in the time while Pilia-Borza extorts the money from Barabas. Ithamore's classicism is meant to seem absurdly out of place:

> Content, but we will leave this paltry land,
> And sail from hence to Greece, to lovely Greece:
> I'll be thy Jason, thou my golden fleece;
> Where painted carpets o'er the meads are hurl'd,
> And Bacchus' vineyards overspread the world,
> Where woods and forests go in goodly green,
> I'll be Adonis, thou shalt be Love's Queen . . . (4.2.83–7)

The fact that Ithamore speaks this language of love may be no more absurd than the discrepancies between Ferneze's rhetoric and actions. More striking similarities develop between the Turkish slave and the Christian Knight. Ithamore offers a shorthand version of Ferneze's pious justifications for attacking Barabas: 'To undo a Jew is charity, and not sin' (4.4.76). He is also like Ferneze in that he too writes short, sharp decrees to extort money.

Barabas has to respond to the written decrees of his former messenger. This is because he placed too much trust in Ithamore, just as Barnardine made the mistake of revealing too much to an accomplice. He retaliates by staging another of his improvisations. It is characteristic that the idea for the improvisation should come to him quickly and that it should be communicated to the audience:

> I have it:
> I will in some disguise go see the slave,
> And how the villain revels with my gold. (4.3.63–5)

It is also characteristic that he should be both inside and outside his own performance as a French musician who calls to entertain Bellamira. His obvious relish for theatrical display differentiates him from Shylock in Shakespeare's *The Merchant of Venice* (?1596–8). Shylock despises the noisy Venetian masqueraders with their painted, or varnished, faces. He becomes the victim of a masque when Portia and Nerissa dress themselves up to improvise the parts of lawyer and clerk in the trial scene. Barabas, by contrast, thrives upon improvisation and masquerade. He is a versatile entertainer who provides pleasure for the spectators. This, by itself, may prevent them from marching away accepting the official script that calls for his punishment and death.

When Bellamira demands the posy of flowers that Barabas is wearing in his hat, he gleefully reveals its significance to the spectators:

> So, now I am reveng'd upon 'em all.
> The scent thereof was death; I poison'd it. (4.4.41–2)

Machiavelli's disciples became infamous for their ingenuity with poison. The Duke of Guise kills Joan, Queen of Navarre, in *The Massacre at Paris* by making her a present of scented gloves which he has poisoned. Barabas in fact slightly miscalculates the amount of poison needed to bring his improvised revenge drama to a successful conclusion. Bellamira, Pilia-Borza and Ithamore only die after they have informed Ferneze of the extent of Barabas's crimes. The Christian ruler has already been responsible, albeit indirectly, for hanging the wrong person. He is only able to arrest Barabas with the help of grotesque characters like Pilia-Borza and Bellamira.

T.S. Eliot describes *The Jew of Malta* in *Selected Essays* (1951) as being a 'farce of the old English humour' (p. 123). The problem with his reading is that terms such as 'farce' and 'caricature' are allowed to float free from political contexts. The staging of farce is one of the ways in which Barabas combats Ferneze's theatre of rule with its emphasis on procession and spectacle. *The Jew of Malta* dramatises a contest between rival playwrights. It also explores the politics of 'caricature' by considering the ownership of propaganda images. Ferneze demonises both Turks and Jews as a way of defining and policing the margins of Maltese society. He enriches himself into the bargain. His exploitation of propaganda makes it acceptable for Bellamira and Pilia-Borza to victimise Barabas. The classical ruler and his grotesque subjects set about the task in remarkably similar ways. *The Jew of Malta* challenges the monologic authority of Christian propaganda by showing how it is used to legitimate economic opportunism. Another challenge takes the form of the provision of alternatives to the caricatures that define the alien stranger in Christian societies. Ithamore may be the Devil's disciple, but Calymath is more chivalrous and courteous than the aristocratic Christian Knights.

Spectators are left to decide whether the play offers a similar alternative to caricature versions of Jewishness. The simplicity of the Three Jews, who just appear at the beginning of the play, only serves to emphasise Barabas's cunning. Abigail has the potential to provide a more positive image of Jewish life and yet is determined to abandon it altogether after Barabas has destroyed her relationship with Mathias. Her representation suggests a related problem with the play's critique of Christian propaganda. She is treated as a commodity by the mercenary Friar Barnardine and yet can also be seen as being a disposable item within the overall structure of the play. Spectators may march away from the theatre believing that some propaganda images have been reproduced rather than replaced. Christians are shown to be every bit as mercenary and opportunistic as Jews. They are more accomplished disciples of Machiavelli. Their authority may be challenged, although their propaganda against Jews nevertheless remains intact. Spectators may alternatively leave the theatre believing that Barabas himself represents positive values that the propaganda seeks to deny. He is a highly versatile entertainer whose improvisations provide theatrical pleasure.

6
Edward II

6.1 Imagining the King's Death

Ralegh used world history as a stage on which he conducts dialogues with his enemies. His description of King Darius of Persia as a player-king can also be read as an attack on King James. History books and plays could raise topical issues which it would have been dangerous to deal with more directly. The past did not become a safe haven for topical, or what the Elizabethans called fustian, allusions for purely strategic reasons. Most Elizabethans believed that history followed cyclical rather than linear patterns. This is not to deny that they had access to different types of historical writing. There were apocalyptic accounts such as John Foxe's *Actes and Monuments* (1563) which raided both past and present for signs that the Millennium, or second coming of Christ, was nigh. Other religious accounts offered more generalised illustrations of divine intervention or providence. History was seen as the theatre of God's judgements. Apocalyptic and providential histories were usually strongly nationalistic, placing England at the centre of the historical struggle for godly rule. There were also an increasing number of nationalistic histories by Camden, Holinshed and others which, while not abandoning the idea of providence, were nevertheless also informed by a range of more secular concerns. The Elizabethan period also produced historians like

John Stow who were concerned with local history. It is therefore dangerous to assume that there was a consensus of opinion about the specific issues that historical writings needed to address. Most Elizabethan historians nevertheless believed that the past was a mirror, or looking glass, which could show either what was happening in the present or what was likely to occur in the future. History was therefore invested with the kind of immediacy and topicality that has become increasingly alien in Western cultures. Plays dealing with historical themes were therefore bound to have a double movement.

Edward II was probably first written and performed in 1592. No information has survived about its early reception. One way of exploring this is to consider the reception of a broadly similar play. Shakespeare's *Richard II* (1595), like *Edward II*, represents the deposition and murder of a monarch. Shakespeare's deposition scene was regarded as being too controversial for publication and was therefore edited out of the early quartos. It may have been the result of self-censorship by the Lord Chamberlain's Men rather than an act of external censorship. The Lord Chamberlain's Men were nevertheless persuaded to revive the play, complete with the deposition scene, on the eve of the Earl of Essex's rebellion in 1601. Essex's failure to perform a dashing part in Ireland, and so retain the Queen's favour, helped to spur him towards rebellion. The Privy Council examined the background to this provocative theatrical event and seems to have been satisfied that the actors were only doing their job. The play may appear to modern spectators to offer a highly ambiguous representation of Bolingbroke's rebellion against Richard and yet, for Elizabethan spectators, any deposition scene provided an opportunity to imagine the unimaginable and to think the unthinkable.

The reception of *Richard II* indicates that a deposition scene was likely to be regarded as controversial. The topicality of history meant that Richard's reign could not be viewed with antiquarian detachment. Indeed, Elizabeth increasingly came to identify herself with Richard and to see the last years of his reign as providing a mirror-image of her own reign. Given the controversy that surrounded *Richard II*, it is surprising that there is no record of any official displeasure with *Edward II*. Such an absence may, of course, be taken as evidence that Marlowe's play was not considered to be as dangerous. The text itself nevertheless provides evidence that it could have been seen as being even more controversial than *Richard II*.

Marlowe's play represents the execution as well as the deposition of a monarch. As has been shown, Barabas is publicly executed in front of both on-stage and theatre spectators at the end of *The Jew of Malta*. Edward's execution is a more private event since it takes place in the lower depths of Berkeley Castle and is only witnessed by the executioner himself and the two gaolers. It is nevertheless transformed into a form of public execution by being staged in front of theatre audiences. Shakespeare's Richard is hastily stabbed to death at Pomfret Castle. Marlowe's Edward, by contrast, dies in a manner that was closer to the spectacles of suffering on the scaffold. Elizabethan spectators were acutely aware that it was high treason to imagine the death of the monarch. Charles Tilney was executed in 1586, along with the other Babington conspirators, for suggesting that Elizabeth might be set upon in her coach.

The staging, or imagining, of the execution of a monarch was a potentially provocative act. The dramatic context for Edward's death nevertheless helps to make this particular scene less controversial. Mortimer, the over-mighty subject who orders the execution, is himself put to death. His claim to have legitimate, patriotic grievances against Edward is shown to be a Machiavellian front. The play ends with Edward's son re-asserting monarchical authority. This orthodox resolution may cover up the subversive act of imagining not just the death, but the public death, of any monarch. The scaffold had always been the place where monarchs displayed their power by punishing their enemies, although they were not necessarily the only members of society who staged executions. It was in fact only in Elizabeth's reign that what Lawrence Stone refers to in *The Crisis of the Aristocracy 1558–1641* (1965) as the royal monopoly of violence became more firmly established. The staging of any executions in playhouses can, perhaps, be seen as a technical infringement of this monopoly. *Edward II* appears to challenge it much more directly by reversing roles. It allows a monarch to play the part of the victim in a spectacle of suffering. This repositioning of the monarch forces the spectators to think hard about their own positions. They are not given detailed instructions about how they ought to respond. Many critics suggest that the play is characterised by the apparently detached, neutral way in which the dialogues over the ethics of deposition and execution are rendered.

The execution scene, like the play as a whole, is based on Holinshed's *Chronicles*. Marlowe generally edits Holinshed's account to such an extent that the events of Edward's reign become bewildering in their rapidity. One of the stage directions indicates that Edward and his followers are '*flying about the stage*' (4.5). The play dramatises the speed and confusion of the historical process, which obviously creates further problems for spectators.

Marlowe nevertheless makes an important exception to his general rule of condensing Holinshed as far as the execution scene is concerned. He extends Holinshed's account of the psychological torture to which Edward is subjected immediately before his death. The two gaolers, Matrevis and Gurney, receive orders from Mortimer to inflict a regime of disorientation and deprivation on him:

> Remove him still from place to place at night,
> And at the last he come to Killingworth,
> And then from thence to Berkeley back again;
> And by the way, to make him fret the more,
> Speak curstly to him; and in any case
> Let no man comfort him, if he chance to weep,
> But amplify his grief with bitter words. (5.2.59–65)

Matrevis and Gurney also develop their own techniques for assailing Edward's mind. They make him stand in an open sewer for days on end. Sewers were inextricably connected with crime and criminality. The Fleet was the name of both a sewer and the prison where Bernard Maude started practising against Catholics. Prisoners in Bridewell had to pull a dungcart through the neighbouring streets. The outcasts in *The Jew of Malta* surprise the city by entering it through the sewers. *Edward II* places a monarch in a space that was associated with grotesque characters who threatened order and stability. It is a potentially provocative reversal of roles. Matrevis and Gurney play 'continually upon a drum' (5.5.60) to deprive Edward of sleep. Dekker indicates in *Villanies Discovered by Lanthorne and Candlelight* (1616) and *Dekker His Dreame* (1620) that incessant noise was a general feature of prison life. The specific reference to the drum nevertheless suggests that Edward is subjected to the kind of orchestrated torture that was reserved for some political prisoners. Marlowe not only elaborates upon Holinshed's account but also includes material from other historians, such as the incident when Matrevis and Gurney shave off Edward's beard which is taken from Stow. The gaolers inflict depersonalisation, as well as disorientation and deprivation. They use 'puddle water' (5.3.30), or sewer water, and act out a grotesque parody of loyal servants attending to the every whim of their master.

The play imagines the execution of the monarch being performed by a hired executioner, which is the most significant addition that it makes to Holinshed's account. Mortimer recruits Lightborn who, like Barabas and Ithamore, prides himself on his evil artistry. The regicide has no blood on his hands:

I learn'd in Naples how to poison flowers;
To strangle with a lawn thrust through the throat;
To pierce the windpipe with a needle's point;
Or whilst one is asleep, to take a quill
And blow a little powder in his ears,
Or open his mouth and pour quicksilver down. (5.4.31–6)

Lightborn reveals his Machiavellian credentials for the task, while at the same time taking care to conceal how he is going to accomplish it. Lightborn(e) appears in *The Fall of Lucifer* (?1467–1488), the first play in the Chester Cycle of mystery plays, as a boastful angel who is banished from Heaven with Lucifer. The executioner is therefore firmly associated with the theatre of Hell. He continues the grotesque parody of master-servant relationships by affecting to be deeply concerned about Edward's welfare. This devil assumes a pleasing shape: 'O speak no more, my lord; this breaks my heart' (5.5.70). Edward may not be convinced by this show of compassion, although he still allows himself to be caressed by Lightborn's rhetoric. He also allows himself to be caressed physically by his executioner. The dungeon would have been represented emblematically rather than naturalistically on the Elizabethan stage. The gaolers give Lightborn a set of keys and a candle. These were probably the only props that were used to establish the setting. Edward may have been placed in the pit that could be created in the stage by opening a trapdoor. The Elizabethan Lightborn may have had to lift and carry Edward to a bed, before lovingly placing him on it.

Lightborn follows the practices of the Elizabethan public executioners by targeting the lower, or grotesque, body. Marlowe moves back to Holinshed's account for the details of this particular execution:

> they came suddenly one night into the chamber where he lay in bed fast asleep, and with heavy featherbeds or a table (as some write) being cast upon him, they kept him down and withall put into his fundament a horn, and through the same they thrust up into his body a hot spit . . . the which passing up into his entrails, and being rolled to and fro, burnt the same, but so as no appearance of any wound or hurt outwardly might be once perceived. His cry did move many within the castle and town of Berkeley to compassion. (HC, 2, p.587)

Twentieth-century productions often tame the execution scene. Bertolt Brecht's version of the play, *The Life of Edward II of England* (1924), allows the King to suffocate to death. Marlowe's text nevertheless makes it clear through the mention of the various props (red-hot spit, table and featherbed) that Elizabethan productions would probably have staged the execution as it was recorded by Holinshed, complete with a death-cry that 'will raise the town' (5.5.113).

The play as a whole is characterised by the speed and confusion of events and yet one of the functions of Lightborn's intimate exchanges with his victim is to slow down the tempo. Edward has time to offer a detailed account of his imprisonment. As the 'lamentable death' of the king was announced in the play's full title and the details of it were reasonably well-known anyway, Marlowe self-consciously makes spectators wait for an expected melodramatic climax. Elizabethan spectators were nevertheless used to much more prolonged spectacles of suffering than Marlowe was able to offer them. Although probably hard for modern spectators to appreciate, the shock value of this scene lies as much in its irony as in its cruelty. The irony is that the play imagines not just the death, but the public execution, of a monarch. It reverses traditional roles so that the monarch becomes a victim in, rather than an instigator of, a theatre of Hell. The royal monopoly on violence is challenged.

6.2 Speaking for England

Some of the difficulties that are created for spectators by the play's compressed, confusing version of history are dramatised through the shifting allegiances of Edward's brother, the Earl of Kent. He starts off by supporting Edward in the power struggle with barons, who were known at the time as the Lords Ordainers. He is then concerned about the damaging effects of Edward's relationship with Piers Gaveston. He therefore joins the barons and, after their defeat, helps Mortimer to escape to France. He returns to England with Mortimer and Queen Isabella's invading army, but immediately begins to question the legitimacy of the enterprise. He fails to prevent Mortimer from seizing power and so decides to rescue Edward from imprisonment. He is taken prisoner and returned to Mortimer, who has him executed. His dilemma about whether to support the weak king or the strong subject may well parallel the shifting allegiances of many spectators as the confusing events of the play rapidly unfold.

The audience's difficulties are intensified by the fact that Marlowe, unlike Shakespeare, does not provide a platform for characters whose Englishness lends some authority either to their actions or to their choric commentaries on events. Alexander Iden, 'a poor esquire of Kent' (5.1.75) kills Jack Cade after the 'monstrous traitor' (4.10.65) has broken into his garden, which can also be seen as the garden of England, in *2 Henry VI* (?1590). The Bastard provides a plain-speaking commentary on political and religious troubles in *King John* (?1594). The Gardener and his Man consider the ways in which the power struggle within the court threatens to destroy the garden of the Commonwealth in *Richard II*. It is not just pastoral characters who appear to speak for England in this play: John of Gaunt laments England's degeneration and the Bishop of Carlisle foretells its discordant future. Shakespeare's critique of courtly intrigue and corruption does not necessarily rule out more optimistic celebrations of Englishness, although they often turn out to be more qualified than some critics recognise. Marlowe's critique of the court is, by contrast, more claustrophobic in its intensity because if offers no alternatives. Some barons, such as Pembroke and Leicester, may behave more honourably than others, but this does not lead them to oppose Mortimer's rise to power.

Edward is eventually captured at Neath Abbey by Mortimer's troops after the invasion. His plan to take sanctuary there is betrayed by a Mower, an emblematic character whose gloomy presence foretells death. The Mower can also be seen as one of the few characters in the play who appears to have no connection with the court. This appearance turns out to be deceptive since he hopes to make a reasonable market by betraying Edward. He expects to be paid for services rendered: 'Your worship, I trust, will remember me?' (4.6.115). He wants to belong to the courtly world in which everyone has their price on their back and so does not speak for an alternative set of values.

A broadly similar incident occurs at the very beginning of the play. Gaveston returns from banishment. He was, incidentally, banished by Edward I, who also expelled the Jews from England. He taunts the spectators:

> Farewell base stooping to the lordly peers;
> My knee shall bow to none but to the King
> As for the multitude, that are but sparks
> Rak'd up in embers of their poverty,
> *Tanti!* I'll fan first on the wind,
> That glanceth at my lips and flieth away. (1.1.18–23)

He then meets members of the 'multitude' in the shapes of Three Poor Men. His contempt for them can be compared with Guise's lofty indifference to the Murderers in *The Massacre at Paris*. One of the Poor Men is a discharged soldier, a familiar figure in the streets of Elizabethan London particularly if the counterfeit ones are included. They offer him their services and are prepared to hang about the court waiting for an answer. They too need to belong to the courtly world in which commodities are bought and sold. This is the only world represented by the play. Gaveston is eventually executed by Warwick, who breaks his promise to the other barons that Gaveston should have safe conduct to one last meeting with Edward. James, who has custody of Gaveston at the time, certainly comments on the dishonourable nature of Warwick's actions. He nevertheless feels that he is powerless to do anything else about it: 'Come fellows, it booted not for us to strive' (3.1.18). The 1990 Royal Shakespeare Company production placed the interval at this point and so made this statement into more of a question for the spectators. Would they have tried to protect Gaveston?

Mortimer claims the right to speak for England and yet his patriotism is, ultimately, shown to be a convenient mask for his self-interest. Just as Ferneze employs theology to justify his seizure of Barabas's goods, so Mortimer uses patriotism to justify his seizure of Edward's crown. He argues the case for lawful revolt against Edward with a view to establishing an elected monarchy, which will be responsive to the wishes of Parliament. His potentially progressive desire to curb Edward's authority is nevertheless part of a regressive plan to prevent new men like Gaveston from supplanting the traditional ruling class. He also claims, as Bolingbroke does in *Richard II*, the right to speak for what Pembroke refers to as 'the common sort' (1.4.92). He argues that Edward can only keep Gaveston in luxury by allowing the common soldiers to remain in poverty:

> . . . his wanton humour grieves not me,
> But this I scorn, that one so basely born
> Should by his sovereign's favour grow so pert,
> And riot it with treasure of the realm
> While soldiers mutiny for want of pay. (1.4.401–5)

Mortimer declares that Gaveston is a 'sly inveigling Frenchman' (1.2.57). He therefore speaks for an England whose traditional hierarchies are threatened by alien strangers. Gaveston himself despises members of the 'multitude', whereas Mortimer becomes their champion. He is, according to Edward, successful at this as 'the people love him well' (2.2.234). The play does not, however, provide further evidence to support this claim since it chooses not to represent 'the people'.

Mortimer's claims to speak for England are initially strengthened because he does not appear to have a purely personal axe to grind against Edward. His estates are not seized, as Bolinbroke's are, to help the royal finances. It is true that Edward refuses to pay the ransom for one of his uncles, but this happens after the battle lines have already been drawn. It confirms rather than creates his opposition and is anyway hardly equivalent to the loss of large estates. The general nature of his grievances, together with his habit of making general statements on behalf of disempowered groups, helps him to establish his credentials as a disinterested patriot. It is, nevertheless, a representation which the play goes on to question. The seizure of Bolingbroke's estates, which violated the laws of succession and the justice of inheritance, gave him a good if by no means perfect case against Richard. Mortimer and his followers have a much weaker case against Edward, although they attempt to strengthen it by transforming Gaveston into the grievance of grievances. Richard's opponents certainly attack the influence of court favourites, but this is only part of their case rather than the sum and substance of it. Mortimer and his supporters may refer to problems in Scotland, Ireland and France and yet they usually contrive to bring the argument back to their obsessive hatred of Gaveston.

Brecht's Mortimer is an intellectual who is, initially, reluctant to enter the political arena. Marlowe's Mortimer, by contrast, appears to be a plain-speaking soldier. He cuts short the speech that Queen Isabella gives on landing in England because he considers it to be too 'passionate':

> Nay Madam, if you be a warrior,
> You must not grow so passionate in speeches. (4.4.15–16)

He assumes the authority to speak for Isabella, here and at other moments in the play, because he believes that her emotional responses have no place in his masculine worlds of politics and the army. She is thus disempowered. This helps to explain why she needs to exchange Edward's rule for Mortimer's protection. There is some doubt about when this exchange takes place, which adds to the play's general air of confusion. Edward and Gaveston taunt her about her relationship with Mortimer, although she continues to protest her innocence. She still affects a love for Edward after she has landed in England with the invading army and yet the vacillating Kent notices that 'Mortimer/And Isabel do kiss while they conspire' (4.5.21–2). After Mortimer's execution, she comes under the authority of her son, now King Edward III, who sends her to the Tower. He rejects her emotional, or 'passionate', appeal in favour of doing what he takes to be his political duty. The play represents the personal as being highly political. Edward uses Isabella when it suits him to do so. He employs her to plead with the barons to revoke the order for Gaveston's banishment. He also sends her on a diplomatic mission to France because the king happens to be her brother. She fails to capitalise on this personal connection and is therefore rejected by her brother as well as by her husband and son. She is a more valuable commodity as far as Mortimer is concerned since her presence helps to purchase legitimacy for the invasion. He still feels the need to stop to her 'passionate' mouth.

Mortimer claims that he merely wishes to preserve a traditional social structure which respects degree and pedigree. He nevertheless makes these claims while he himself is advancing from relative obscurity to a position in which his mouth is to all intents and purposes the Parliament of England. He is not an earl at the beginning of the play. His protests about Gaveston's lack of pedigree are a form of self-criticism, which may explain why they become so obsessive. Gaveston is attacked and finally killed for being an alien stranger, yet his desire to rise in the world is no different from the wishes of his enemies. Mortimer, the scourge of favourites, opens his own favour bank immediately after he has defeated Edward: 'Mine enemies will I plague, my friends advance' (5.4.67). These friends include the basely-born Matrevis and Gurney, who replace more nobly-born gaolers:

> As thou intend'st to rise by Mortimer,
> Who now makes Fortune's wheel turn as he please,
> Seek all the means thou canst to make him droop,
> And neither give him kind word nor good look. (5.2.52–5)

Gurney not only carries out Mortimer's plans for psychological torture, but also acts on the order to kill Lightborn immediately after the execution. Lightborn boasts of his Machiavellian cunning only to find himself outwitted by the more secretive Mortimer. The small bird of prey has not noticed the shadow of a larger one. Mortimer nevertheless finds himself outwitted in turn by Gurney, who attempts to buy the friendship of the new king by confessing his crimes. Gurney has a smack of Robert Poley about him. He turns out to be the true disciple of Machiavelli. The seemingly large bird of prey underestimates the apparently smaller one. The *Tamburlaine* plays refuse to acknowledge that pride must go before a fall. *Edward II* is more conventional in showing how the boastful Mortimer is ultimately broken on Fortune's wheel. He sounds like Tamburlaine when he declares his invincibility:

> As for myself, I stand as Jove's huge tree,
> And others are but shrubs compared to me;
> All tremble at my name, and I fear none; . . . (5.6.11–13)

He is nevertheless condemned to death moments later, just as the Guise in *The Massacre at Paris* is murdered immediately after his declaration of immortality.

Mortimer despises Gaveston and yet boasts about his own rise to power. He forces Edward to abdicate and then advances his own favourites. His claim to speak for the people and to protect their constitutional rights is undermined by the way in which he increasingly becomes just like his enemies. Spectators can, if they wish, believe that in the new king they have at last found a character who speaks for England. They can, alternatively, see him as merely representing the mixture as before. His rejection of Isabella certainly follows a pattern that has already been established. The play ends not with Edward's funeral itself, but merely with the preparations for it. The ending thus self-consciously breaks, or disrupts, a ceremony that might have been used to provide a more harmonious resolution.

6.3 The Pursuit of Pleasure

Mortimer believes that he can control 'Fortune's wheel'. Fortune, according to Machiavelli and others, is a woman who sometimes needs to be bullied into submission. Mortimer claims that his *virtú* can control Fortune in much the same way as it has mastered the 'passionate' Isabella. His sense of *virtú* also leads him to oppose those men whom he sees as being effeminate. He insists, as does Tamburlaine, that soldiers must fight against forms of effeminacy.

Mortimer congratulates himself on his Machiavellian cunning immediately after he has sent Lightborn to execute Edward. He takes pleasure in the fact that he is feared rather than loved. He also enjoys recalling how he has fooled even his own supporters with his theatrical tricks:

> They thrust upon me the Protectorship,
> And sue to me for that I desire:
> While at the council-table, grave enough
> And not unlike a bashful puritan,
> First I complain of imbecility, . . . (5.4.56–60)

He gets power by appearing to refuse it. This celebration of theatricality contradicts his earlier critiques of Edward and Gaveston's highly theatrical behaviour. He begins by exhibiting a puritanical dislike of theatre and then reveals that the 'bashful puritan' is just one of the parts in his own dramatic repertoire. *The Jew of Malta* shows how Ferneze's understated performances in the theatre of politics eventually triumph over Barabas's more overstated ones. *Edward II* plays a variation on the same theme by allowing Mortimer's covert performances to triumph, albeit briefly, over Edward and Gaveston's more overt ones. Mortimer turns out to be a counterfeit soldier, since he is an actor who merely plays this part when it suits him to do so.

Holinshed makes a special point of dwelling upon the defects of Edward's education because, if similar mistakes were made with a modern prince, then the cycle of history might well repeat itself. Edward counterfeits kingly virtues for a time and yet is unable to sustain the performance. Holinshed follows earlier histories of the reign in showing how Edward's lack of training for his role ultimately led him into the pursuit of pleasure:

> he gave himself to wantons, passing his time in voluptuous pleasure, and riotous excess: and to help them forward in that kind of life, the foresaid Piers . . . furnished his court with companies of jesters, ruffians, flattering parasites, musicians, and other vile and naughty ribalds, that the king might spend both days and nights in jesting, playing, blanketing, and in such other filthy and dishonourable exercises . . . (HC,2, p. 547)

The play borrows some of these details which then acquire topical, or Elizabethan, associations. Perhaps Mortimer, dressed in Elizabethan costume, reminded spectators of contemporary preachers when he attacked theatrical excess. If so, then the revelation that he is also an actor undermines the authority of this position. He pursues, or attacks, the very pleasures which he also pursues, or in which he indulges.

Gaveston dreams on his return from banishment about how he will transform the court into a palace of pleasures in which he will be the master of ceremonies:

> I must have wanton poets, pleasant wits,
> Musicians, that with touching of a string
> May draw the pliant King which way I please;
> Music and poetry is his delight:
> Therefore I'll have Italian masques by night,
> Sweet speeches, comedies, and pleasing shows; . . .(1.1.60–5)

The master of ceremonies will master the 'pliant King'. Some critics suggest that Edward's relationship with Gaveston is based on a genuine affection, which is unable to survive in the jealous and mercenary atmosphere of the court. Edward certainly believes passionately that Gaveston 'loves me more than all the world' (1.4.77). The relationship can, alternatively, be seen as the product of the court. Edward buys Gaveston's love by showering him with gifts and titles, in much the same way as Jupiter promises to reward Ganymede in *Dido, Queen of Carthage*. He repeats the process, immediately after Gaveston's death, with his new favourties, Spencer and Baldock. He also at one point attempts to buy off the barons by granting them offices and titles. He even tries to buy Lightborn with the one jewel that he has left. Gaveston, like Spencer and Baldock, knows enough about the patronage system to be able to manipulate the king. The fact that both interpretations of the relationship are possible provides yet another example of how the play delights in placing its spectators in ambiguous positions.

Mortimer's sense of *virtù* is offended by the open display of passion between Edward and Gaveston. They play glorious reconciliation scenes and tearful parting scenes, both of which involve a lot of bodily contact. They sit entwined together on the throne and walk about leaning on each others' shoulders. Edward also exhibits this kind of physicality with some of the other characters. He and Isabella kiss, embrace and hold hands in front of the barons as a way of demonstrating their reconciliation. He then embraces at least one of the barons. He also embraces Spencer in front of the Herald as a way of conveying a message to his enemies that he will not change 'His sports, his pleasures, and his company' (3.2.175). He has his head in the Abbot's lap when the mercenary Mower leads Mortimer's troops to him. He does not resist Lightborn's caresses. His open physicality differentiates him from the barons whose stage presences are defined by the way in which they prefer to avoid displays of bodily contact. Mortimer's relationship with Isabella is closed and secretive. They are loath to lay themselves open to each other or anybody else.

Mortimer complains that Gaveston's 'idle triumphs, masques, lascivious shows' (2.2.156) have helped to bankrupt the country. The text itself does not contain any of these theatrical entertainments, although they were probably inserted at the beginning of some of the earlier scenes on the Elizabethan stage. Playwrights who provide entertainment for spectators usually meet violent deaths in Marlowe's plays. Gaveston is beheaded in a ditch. Barabas is boiled alive in a cauldron. As will be seen, Faustus stages plays to entertain his patrons and friends, as well as the spectators, and is then dismembered by Devils. The Guise in *The Massacre at Paris* choreographs the theatre of violence, making sure that the 'actors in this massacre' (4.28) perform the parts that he has written for them. He is eventually stabbed to death.

The text does nevertheless indicate the ways in which Gaveston uses costume to fashion himself into a theatrical spectacle for both Edward's visual pleasure and that of the spectators. Mortimer, ironically as it turns out, despises this theatrical re-presentation of self:

> He wears a lord's revenue on his back,
> And Midas-like he jets it in the court
> With base outlandish cullions at his heels,
> Whose proud fantastic liveries make such show
> As if that Proteus, god of shapes, appear'd. (1.4.406–10)

Renaissance writers like Giovanni Pico della Mirandella set the Proteus myth in the context of optimistic arguments about the individual's potential for change. The actor's Protean abilities to change 'shapes' and therefore to be inconstant was, by contrast, one of the reasons why Elizabethan moralists feared the theatre. As already suggested, actors therefore had to wear the livery of a member of the aristocracy to prevent themselves from being treated, or rather mistreated, as vagrant persons and masterless men. According to Mortimer, Gaveston is a peasant actor who is licensed to play the part of a lord. Gaveston adds insult to this injury by encouraging his own followers to flaunt themselves and so flout social hierarchies. As suggested, such critiques of the theatre usually extended to the stage-play world as costumes were seen as allowing unthrifty knaves to assume the shapes of old soldiers and an anarchic host of other characters. The existing sumptuary legislation failed to prevent what Philip Stubbes refers to in *The Anatomy of Abuses* (1583) as 'a confuse mingle mangle of apparell' (p. 34). Mortimer's critique of Gaveston is highly topical because it is rooted in these specifically late Elizabethan debates about fashion and fashioning. His related outbursts against favourites must also have seemed very familiar to London spectators who followed the fortunes of Ralegh, Essex, Hatton and the others who devoted themselves to gaining and retaining, Her Majesty's pleasure.

Mortimer despises passion and yet becomes passionate about Gaveston's behaviour. He is particularly angry at the way in which Gaveston is licensed, like a court fool, to laugh at the costumes of the other characters:

> Whiles others walk below, the King and he
> From out a window laugh at such as we,
> And flaunt our train, and jest at our attire. (1.4.415–17)

Mortimer, dressed either very plainly or else as a soldier, rages against the way in which Gaveston has transformed Edward into the shape of a player king:

> And then thy soldiers marched like players
> With garish robes, not armour; and thyself,
> Bedaub'd with gold, rode laughing at the rest,
> Nodding and shaking of thy spangled crest,
> Where women's favours hung like labels down. (2.2.182–6)

The reference to 'women's favours' shows that Mortimer despises Edward for being, in his terms, effeminate. He voices, here and elsewhere, Machiavelli's arguments in *Discourses* about the ways in which military and social discipline are essential to prevent both the individual body and the body politic from becoming effeminate. English justice voiced similar views. J.A.Sharpe's *Crime in Early Modern England 1550–1750* (1984) quotes the case of John Taylor of Chester, who was publicly punished in 1608 'for wearing women's apparell'. His sentence reads: 'his clothes to be cut and breeches to be made of them & to be whipped through the city tomorrow' (p. 178). John Rainoldes and others would have liked to have seen actors being dealt with in the same way. Perhaps, if they had been there, they would have applauded Tamburlaine when he kills the effeminate Calyphas.

Gaveston wore lavish, Italianate costumes on the Elizabethan stage. The text refers to his 'Italian hooded cloak' (1.4.412) and 'Tuscan cap' (1.4.413). Such costumes became increasingly fashionable during the 1590s, much to the annoyance of those with vested interests in the English clothing industries. The play associates colour, spectacle and visual pleasure with continental Europe, whereas England stands for all that is plain and repressive. The contrast should be particularly marked at the opening as Gaveston makes his dazzling entrance at a court which is dressed in mourning. The play not only refuses to provide a character who speaks for England with any conviction, but also offers, in the splendid shape(s) of Gaveston, a character who speaks very eloquently against England and Englishness. Gaveston despises the barons because they can only gain pleasure by continually reminding themselves and others of their social superiority:

> Base leaden earls that glory in your birth,
> Go sit at home and eat your tenants' beef,
> And come not here to scoff at Gaveston,
> Whose mounting thoughts did never creep so low,
> As to bestow a look on such as you. (2.2.74–8)

Gaveston glories in himself rather than his birth. He may appear to be remarkably unlike Tamburlaine and yet they both conduct their own very different campaigns against hereditary principles.

Edward licenses Gaveston not only to jest at the barons' attire, but also to strip the Bishop of Coventry of his 'sacred garments' (1.2.25). The Bishop, who is also the Papal Legate, had been involved in Gaveston's original banishment. Costume becomes the battleground on which Edward and his enemies fight each other early on in the play. This incident is taken by the barons as a clear indication that Edward is unfit to rule. Elizabethan spectators may have had more ambiguous responses to it because of the Bishop's connections with Rome. Reformation writers such as John Bale transformed King John into a Protestant hero as a result of his stand against the Pope. Edward is also allowed to speak for Protestant England in a soliloquy, after the Archbishop of Canterbury has threatened to excommunicate him if he does not banish Gaveston:

> Why should a king be subject to a priest?
> Proud Rome, that hatchest such imperial grooms,
> For these thy superstitious taper-lights
> Wherewith thy antichristian churches blaze,
> I'll fire thy crazed buildings, and enforce
> The papal towers to kiss the lowly ground; . . . (1.4.96–101)

The play did not make it easy for Elizabethan spectators to find a settled position from which to interpret the fate of the Bishop of Coventry. Edward takes pleasure in allowing Gaveston to pursue the ritual humiliation of the Bishop. As the Bishop is closely identified with Rome, spectators were invited to share this pleasure. The double movement of the play nevertheless also allows the humiliation to be seen as an attack on Elizabethan religious institutions. Some spectators probably shared the anxieties of the barons about Edward's fitness to govern, whereas others might have enjoyed seeing a character associated with sexual repression stripped almost naked on stage.

Bodies and their costumes visualise the play's political conflicts. These conflicts are also embodied in the language itself. Mortimer likes to play the part of a disciplined man of few words. He tells Isabella at one point that actions speak louder than words. He believes that both 'passionate' and lamenting speeches have no place in his manly world. Ironically, he speaks very passionately against Gaveston. Edward, by contrast, speaks passionately throughout the play. As can be seen, his critique of the Papacy takes the form of an angry curse. His smouldering rage was brought out very effectively by Ian McKellen in the 1969 Prospect Theatre Company production, which formed a double bill with Shakespeare's *Richard II*. Edward is, in the terms of the play, brooked and baited by the barons. He has to make requests and his speeches are frequently interrupted. It is only when he is either alone, or with Gaveston, that he is able to indulge himself rhetorically. Gaveston's position as both the subject of, and the sympathetic audience for, Edward's angry outbursts is quickly filled by Spencer and Baldock. These new favourites are present when Edward kneels down and curses the barons for killing Gaveston:

> If I be England's king, in lakes of gore
> Your headless trunks, your bodies will I trail,
> That you may drink your fill, and quaff in blood,
> And stain my royal standard with the same; . . . (3.2.135–8)

Edward's anger usually prompts him to prophesy devastation and destruction. He threatens to burn churches to the ground and to cover his realm with 'lakes of gore'. He vows to pursue those who stop his pursuit of pleasure.

6.4 When Regiment is Gone

The deposition scene, like the execution scene, depends upon irony. As noted, the irony at the heart of the execution scene is that roles are reversed to allow a monarch to suffer a form of public execution. The irony in the deposition scene also relies upon reversal. It is probably the first time in the play that Edward both behaves, and is allowed to behave, like a king. He becomes like a king when it is too late. He is, ironically, given a chance to command the stage only when it is time for him to exit from it. He begins to assert his authority when, to all intents and purposes, he has none. His performance is essentially much ado about nothing. Leicester is, at this point, Edward's gaoler. Winchester and Trussel have been delegated by Parliament to receive the crown. All three of them confine themselves to short statements. Their content may not, at times, be deferential but Edward is neverthe-less addressed correctly throughout. There were occasions earlier on when Mortimer and others defiantly refused to use the correct modes of address such as 'Your Grace' and 'My Lord'. Edward was also irritated by the way in which some of his over-mighty subjects refused to kneel before him. The etiquette in the deposition scene is exemplary and yet Edward has to resign his right to expect such deference. He is at last given the opportunity to make the kind of speeches which were only possible before either as soliloquies, or else in the company of his favourites. He appears to have world enough and time to explain why kings are different from their subjects:

> The griefs of private men are soon allay'd,
> But not of kings: the forest deer being struck
> Runs to an herb that closeth the wounds,
> But when the imperial lion's flesh is gor'd
> He rends and tears it with his wrathful paw,
> And highly scorning that the lowly earth
> Should drink his blood, mounts up into the air: . . . (5.1.8–14)

He is, ironically, about to become a very private man.

He plays, or acts, the part of a king to perfection, perhaps because he too is conscious that he is only being allowed to give a performance:

> But what are kings, when regiment is gone,
> But perfect shadows in a sunshine day?
> My nobles rule, I bear the name of king;
> I wear the crown; but am controll'd by them, . . . (5.1.26–9)

He does not however just become an actor, or shadow, when his authority, or 'regiment', is taken away. He has always been a player king, perhaps most notably when he acts out the reconciliation scene with Isabella and the barons. He has also been a king who could not live without the visual pleasures offered by shows and spectacles. These are the reasons why Mortimer forces him to act out a deposition scene. His speeches, which are by turns lofty, angry and self-pitying, dominate the stage from which he nevertheless has to exit. Like both Tamburlaine and Faustus, he is unable to make time stand still. The stage is required by another actor who wants to use it to play the 'bashful puritan' and the English patriot.

Modern criticism tends to emphasise the emotional rather than ironic impact of both the deposition and execution scenes. It asks whether Edward becomes a more 'sympathetic' character in defeat and death. As such questions are raised, it is only fair to try to answer them even though they deflect attention away from the play's specifically Elizabethan qualities. Modern audiences might find it difficult to sympathise with Edward because his downfall does not appear to produce self-knowledge. One of the changes that Brecht made to Marlowe's play was to allow Edward to become more conscious of his faults. Marlowe is not so concerned with the development of character. Edward replaces one favourite with others. The deposition scene contains examples of the rage that surfaced earlier on in the curses against Rome and the barons. The execution scene shows that he is still receptive to flattery. Reviews of modern productions suggest that the question of sympathy may also be complicated for some spectators by Edward's sexuality. The question of sympathy for him ultimately becomes part of a larger one about responses to the pleasures that he pursues.

As noted, Elizabethan propaganda demonised the 'sodomite' as somebody who must also be a threat to Church and State. It is possible to see Edward as conforming to this construction. He allows the Bishop of Coventry to be defrocked and helps to plunge the country into civil war. If this is so, then the play follows the themes of *The Jew of Malta* and confronts spectators with their own demons. There is a particularly savage irony about the way in which it is the ruler himself who has many of the characteristics of the alien stranger. Those who want to condemn Edward for his sexuality are not allowed the easy option of attacking a marginalised figure. They are forced to attack the most central figure of all. Those who want to condemn Edward also have to come to terms with the fact that it is he and Gaveston who provide visual and theatrical pleasure in an otherwise drab and hostile environment.

Such readings are possible, although the essential point about the play's treatment of homosexuality is perhaps that it is allowed to become a subject for dialogue and debate in the first place. Lancaster echoes the official propaganda: '*Diablo!* What passions call you these?' (1.4.318). Just as Sir Christopher Hatton demonised Catholicism by referring to it as being '*diabolica*', so Lancaster is unable to find English words with which to express his disgust. Mortimer Senior takes a more tolerant attitude by setting

Edward's relationship with Gaveston within classical contexts and thus to some extent normalising it. Mortimer himself affects to be untroubled by Edward's 'wanton humour', although is sorely troubled by the social gulf between Edward and Gaveston. The play creates some space for a dialogue with Elizabethan propaganda by offering a range of responses to homosexuality. It also allows Edward and Gaveston to express their own views in their declarations of love for each other.

As mentioned, critics have suggested that the play is neutral rather than sympathetic in its treatment of both Edward and the barons. Neutrality should never be treated as a neutral term. It became associated in Victorian England with forms of political and economic liberalism. It is harder to work out what its political associations might have been in Elizabethan England. It is nevertheless clear that Elizabethans were not encouraged to be neutral on burning issues which involved the Church and State. Legislation was used to prevent what was known as diversity in opinions. One of the persistent arguments against the theatre, which was repeated by the Privy Council in a letter to the Archbishop of Canterbury dated 12 November 1589, was that players were taking it upon themselves to handle and therefore offer their own interpretations of theological and political matters. Neutrality, or the practice of initiating dialogues which remain unresolved, was a controversial position to both adopt and encourage others to adopt. Marlowe's seemingly neutral stance can therefore be seen as being a potentially provocative and radical one. The play is nevertheless remarkably traditional in other respects. It is written from above in the sense that it concentrates exclusively on courtly intrigues and power struggles. The barons are sharply criticised by Gaveston for being parochial and yet the play itself can be seen as being almost as limited in its own range. Those who are placed below the court are only given a tokenistic presence to illustrate the pervasive nature of courtly values. They exist off-stage as raw material that can be fashioned by unscrupulous politicians like Mortimer, who claim the right to speak for England. Yet they also formed the audience for a play that encouraged them to debate such controversial subjects as punishment, deposition and homosexuality.

7
Doctor Faustus

7.1 Sacred and Profane Texts

There are two versions of *Doctor Faustus*. The first one, known as
the A-Text, was published in 1604. It was probably a reprint of a
1601 edition. There have been a number of theories as to why it is
shorter than comparable texts. William Empson suggests in
Faustus and the Censor (1987) that the original text was censored
because it contained monstrous opinions. Most other critics prefer
more purely theatrical explanations. It has been argued that the
A-text might represent the play as it was staged on a provincial
tour by a small company without the facilities, such as a gallery
and stage machinery, that were more readily available in the
London public theatres. There is also the view that the length of
this text can be explained by the fact that it was reconstructed with
the aid of either a prompt-book, or else an actor's memory. It is
argued that such sources usually produced a text that was shorter
than the play in performance.

The second version, known as the B-text, was published in 1616
and is the text that is being used here. It is substantially longer
than the A-text. Some of the new material increases the comic
nature of the scenes set in Rome, the Court of Charles the Fifth
and Vanholt. It also provides Faustus with more opportunities to
display his magical powers and calls for elaborate stage effects

such as the descent of the heavenly throne near the end of the play. The B-text includes a scene in which the Scholars discover Faustus's body after it has been dismembered by the Devils. This scene, according to Empson, increases the play's orthodoxy by emphasising the material reality of Hell and its existence can therefore be related to the censorship question. If the A-text is seen as the script after censorship, then the B-text becomes a script that includes some of the amendments by the Master of Revels.

There are, once again, theories which concentrate on more purely theatrical explanations for the differences between the two versions of the play. If the A-text is seen as a suitable script for provincial performances by a relatively small company, then the B-text can become the one that was used in the London play-houses. It is impossible to answer the question of whether the new material in the B-text had its origins in the 1590s, or took the form of later additions. Some critics have argued in favour of a close relationship between the B-text and a lost original version of the play.

The debate over these two texts is complicated by the fact that there are important gaps in the play's stage history. The first recorded performances of *Doctor Faustus* took place in the autumn of 1594 at The Rose Theatre, although it is clear that it was no longer a new play by then. It was nevertheless still a successful one and remained in the repertoire until 1597. There were plans to revive it in 1602 as two writers were paid for making additions to it. The nature of these additions, and the question of whether or not they were incorporated into the B-text, must remain matters for speculation. Some critics date the first perfor-mance of the play relatively early in Marlowe's career, after the *Tamburlaine* plays. Others argue in favour of a date either at, or towards, the end of it.

Further problems are caused by the Faust Books which critics, in a rare moment of agreement, acknowledge to have been Marlowe's main source. *The Historie of the Damnable Life and Deserved Death of Doctor John Faustus*, usually just referred to as the English Faust-Book, was published in 1592. It was a transla-tion of the German Faust-Book, which first appeared in 1587. The copy that has survived is not, however, a first edition. Those who prefer the earlier date for *Doctor Faustus* are therefore not bound to accept that it must have been written and first performed in, or after, 1592. The evidence nevertheless suggests that the lost first edition of the English Faust-Book may also have been published sometime in 1592. Yet this by itself does not necessarily rule out an early date for *Doctor Faustus*. Empson notes that the German Faust-Book was 'one of the first international best sellers, translated into six languages of Western Europe in as many years' (p.1). Perhaps Marlowe had access either to an edition, or a manuscript, that pre-dated the publication of the English Faust-Book. A later date for the play, probably 1592, nevertheless seems to fit the evidence that has survived.

The debates about the textual and stage history of *Doctor Faustus* are more complex, and certainly more heated, than has been suggested here. Partisan preferences for one of the texts can, nevertheless, often obscure central questions. Why, for instance, are arguments about textual authenticity and originality considered to be so vital? Faustus himself hopes that magic will resolve all of the 'ambiguities' (1.1.78) that perplex his scholarly mind. This quest is often condemned by modern scholars who nevertheless still want to resolve most, if not all, of the play's textual problems. It can be argued that such a desire for resolution is only natural given the difficulties. Yet the terms that are often used in this particular quest for certainty are highly political ones. Critics tend to search for a coherent, consistent and unified text which can be attributed to a single author. Those parts of the text which do not appear to conform to this view of authorship are often dismissed as being, to quote from the debates themselves, debasements, adulterations, corruptions, vulgarisations, intrusions and contaminations.

Such a polarisation between the coherent and the contaminated text is often based upon modern rather than Renaissance concepts of theatrical authorship. Elizabethan companies tended to publish a play as a way of registering and therefore protecting copyright. The playwrights may have been concerned to have volumes of poetry published under their own names, although they generally showed relatively little interest in what happened to their plays. These were viewed as the property of the company, rather than as their own special creation. The quest to identify Marlowe's, or Shakespeare's, voice is often related to modern political anxieties about the anarchy which is associated with murmuring, mingling and multiple voices.

The comic scenes in *Doctor Faustus* are usually held to lack Marlowe's coherent, poetic voice. Similar concerns have been expressed about the last three acts of *The Jew of Malta*. Elizabethan comedy was certainly the product of collaboration. This could take the form of the dramatist's original script being filled out by the clowns with their own routines and gags. It could also take the form of clowns improvising an entire scene. Who controls such scenes? It is possible to opt for a combination of author and actor. Another answer would be the spectators themselves whose laughter, or lack of it, ultimately determines the script. It still has to be said, however, that those who claim that Marlowe would never have contaminated his own scripts with comedy are airing their own prejudices about the nature of a sacred and a profane text.

John D. Jump's Introduction to the Revels edition of *Doctor Faustus* (1968), which is still used by students, provides a good example of how anxieties about authorship can distort critical practice. Comedy is placed towards the bottom of the agenda, a long way after a very good summary of textual problems and just before some concluding remarks on stage history:

> The farcical prose scenes call for a little attention. . . . No doubt there is a touch of crude burlesque in such places. But the current critical fashion ordains that we should go further and discern in them a profound, subtle, and sustained irony. We shall do well to remember that there is a limit to the violence that we are entitled to do to common sense in the name of literary criticism. (pp. 1vii–1viii)

Jump constructs an opposition between 'fashion', which is proverbially changeable and followed blindly, and the voice of 'common sense', which derives its authority through its apparent detachment. The bad critical angels support coercion, 'violence' and distortion of the evidence. The good critical angels champion reason and toleration.

Jump fails to acknowledge that critics who recognise the importance of the comic scenes may, in fact, be trying to follow Renaissance rather than contemporary fashions. Renaissance societies allowed those who belonged to the culture of the university to participate as well in the culture of the market place.

Rabelais's writings provide the best example of the ways in which Humanism and 'crude burlesque' were neither mutually exclusive worlds nor styles. *Doctor Faustus*, an adaptation of a best-seller credited to a popular dramatist who had spent six years at university, combines the serious and the crude in ways that would not have seemed alien to Renaissance spectators. Indeed, one way of reading the play is to see Faustus himself as moving from the university to the market place. Jump's 'common sense' is therefore in danger of distorting a historical sense of *Doctor Faustus*. Those critics who see the play as still being essentially medieval in its construction might want to argue that Jump's pronouncements also distort the relationship between the serious and the comic in medieval cultures.

There are at least three possible responses to the question of whether it matters who wrote which parts of *Doctor Faustus*. The first, and probably the best, answer is to ignore textual debates altogether in order to concentrate on readings or dramatisations of one of the available texts. The second answer, which has been sketched in here, is to say that the debates matter because they reveal some of the assumptions that are often smuggled into criticism in the name of 'common sense'. A third, and less controversial, answer is to acknowledge that, although the main questions remain unanswerable, the fact that they are posed has nevertheless led to the discovery of some valuable details about Renaissance theatrical practices. To take just one example, the A-text refers to a Doctor Lopus, or Lopez. As already noted, Lopez's trial and execution were major political events in 1594. The Horse-Courser refers to them when he laments buying a horse from Faustus:

> Alas, alas, Doctor Fustian, quotha! Mass, Doctor Lopus was
> never such a doctor. H'as given me a purgation, h'as purged me`
> of forty dollars: I shall never see them more. (4.4.37–9)

This topical allusion provides a good example of how theatrical scripts were doctored to retain their popularity. The shorthand manner in which this speech is rendered retains the feel of an improvisation. The reference to Lopez could not have been written by Marlowe. It is not included in the B-text. Some critics would argue that this is because this text is much closer to

Marlowe's original version. Others who favour a later date might point out that this allusion was dropped from performance when it had lost its topicality and no longer got a laugh. Its inclusion in the A-text provides an important reminder of the collaborative way in which Renaissance drama texts were produced. Ironically, the quest by textual critics to identify Marlowe's voice has unearthed a lot of evidence about collaborative forms of authorship. This sometimes gets buried again because the debates about the two texts are concerned to identify the sacred text that can be attributed to a single author.

7.2 The Quiet House and the Solitary Grove

The Prologue confronts spectators by appearing to deny them conventional theatrical pleasures. The play that they have paid to see will not display heroic themes or locations. It will confine itself to the story of a German scholar. The tone is provocative and the content is misleading. Spectators who had either read, or just heard about, the Faust-Book would have known that this story included, if not conventional battle scenes, then at least representations of both exotic locations and 'the dalliance of love' (1.3) in the form of Faustus's relationship with Helen of Troy.

The Faust-Book became a best-seller because it promised to make exclusive worlds more inclusive. Readers are not only drawn inside a magic circle, but are also allowed access to other secret societies. They accompany Faustus into the Pope's private chamber and are present when he enters the equally exclusive world of the Turkish harem. They are taken on a number of guided tours, visiting the main attractions in Rome as well as making a flying visit to Hell. The text nevertheless offers the security of the familiar alongside the excitements of the unfamiliar. The tourists may lose sight of knowable landmarks, such as the tavern or the market place, and yet they are always transported back to this familiar world. Perhaps they never really leave it given the vernacular tone of their guidebook. The trip to Rome lets them view new locations and confirm old prejudices. The Faust-Book allowed readers to experience the shock of the new without denying them the reassurances of the old.

The Prologue begins by making the story of 'Faustus' fortunes, good or bad' (1.8) sound unexciting in comparison with both the Faust-Book itself and popular theatre in general. It then makes an unpromising appeal to the 'patient judgements' (1.9) of the spectators. It is only at the end of a patient reconstruction of Faustus's life that it is revealed that he 'surfeits upon cursed necromancy' (1.25). Faustus is represented as displaying a sensual attitude to all forms of knowledge. He has glutted, or surfeited, himself on sacred as well as profane texts. He desires knowledge because it will in turn allow him to feed other desires. The Prologue, or homily, may establish this interpretation and yet it also seems to go out of its way to deny some of the popular pleasures associated with the Faust-Book. Perhaps it wants to suggest that there is a form of theatrical pleasure in being made to wait for pleasure. Spectators are therefore immediately placed in ambiguous positions. They have to listen to a homily against sensuality before they can indulge their own senses by watching the play's own surfeit of spectacle and listening to its mighty lines. A conventional way of reading the play is to see it as beginning and ending well, but as falling away in the middle because Marlowe's voice is held to be not so clearly audible here. This may underestimate the problematic nature of the opening for those Elizabethan spectators who had come to be entertained.

Faustus is no longer content to inhabit the study in what the Chorus to Act Three refers to as his 'quiet house' (15). His books have become a source of irritation rather than pleasure. Aristotle is tossed aside on the grounds that he is only capable of teaching the techniques of dispute. Ironically, Faustus goes on to demonstrate his mastery of the technique of selective quotation. The medical writings of Galen are rejected because they do not feed Faustus's own vanity. They may allow him to prevent 'whole cities' (1.1.21) from being destroyed by the plague and yet they still remind him of his own mortality. The first recorded performances of *Doctor Faustus* took place just after London had been stalked by the plague, which probably killed at least eleven thousand people. Faustus's casual rejection of his own medical skills must have shocked many spectators. The legal writings of Justinian also conjure up what is seen to be a world of petty drudgery in the service of others. Faustus easily convinces himself, if not his audience, that the Bible only offers the prospect of 'everlasting death' (1.1.44) for sinners.

Faustus's sacred texts are 'necromantic books' (1.1.48) which hold out the promise of personal power, pleasure and profit. He therefore caresses them, just as Barabas fondles his bags of gold, instead of casting them petulantly aside. He sends for the magicians, Valdes and Cornelius, so that he can share his imperial fantasies with them. Valdes claims that magic can transform the 'quiet house' into a version of Barabas's counting house by conjuring up spirits who will ransack the world of wealth:

> From Venice shall they drag huge argosies,
> And from America the golden fleece
> That yearly stuffs old Philip's treasure,
> If learned Faustus will be resolute. (1.1.128–31)

These fantasies, together with Faustus's earlier desire to defeat the Prince of Parma, reveal the kind of anti-Spanish prejudices that were commonplace on the Elizabethan stage. The spectators are put in a difficult position. Faustus and his friends are, at one and the same time, indulging in unorthodox practices and voicing some of the orthodoxies of Elizabethan propaganda and policy. Ralegh and others were officially commissioned to annoy Philip II by diverting wealth away from his treasury. John Savage and some of the other Babington conspirators had served with Parma in the Low Countries.

Valdes and Cornelius confirm Faustus's desire to practise magic. Edward Alleyn apparently wore a surplice with a cross on it when he created the part of Faustus to ward off the dangerous consequences of raising devils on stage. The spectators had no such protection. Stories began to circulate about real devils being raised. Modern spectators might want to read such stories as being good publicity, or hype. Some Elizabethan spectators may well have taken the same attitude to them, although others would have read them much more literally. Michael Hattaway suggests in *Elizabethan Popular Theatre: Plays in Performance* (1982) that what these stories

> indicate is that the Elizabethans found the play *frightening*, an occasion for collective exotic *frissons*. For them it was the

spectacle of the devils and not the mind of the hero that was at the centre of the play. (p.167)

Although this may overstate the case, it nevertheless recovers important aspects of the play's reception on the Elizabethan stage.

Faustus is urged to find a 'solitary grove' (1.1.151) outside Wittenberg in which to perform his incantations. He thus evades the surveillance of the city authorities, while openly displaying subversive secrets to the spectators. He instructs them on how to raise devils:

> Within this circle is Jehovah's name
> Forward and backward anagrammatiz'd:
> Th'abbreviated names of holy saints,
> Figures of every adjunct to the heavens,
> And characters of signs and erring stars
> By which the spirits are enforc'd to rise. (1.3.8–13)

His actions can be seen as being broadly similar to those of the Elizabethan actors and dramatists who established their own solitary groves, or public theatres, in the Liberties of London. The ambiguous nature of such a location meant that they too could sometimes reveal secrets at the same time as they were concealing them.

Faustus is a solitary figure who disputes with himself. He not only frequents marginal places like the grove, but also holds a marginal place within society itself. His education has cut him off from family ties. Like Tamburlaine and Gaveston, his parents are of the commoner sort. His house is 'quiet' because he lives there alone with only the servants for company. He also appears to be outside the university's jurisdiction. One of the Scholars declares an intention to inform the Rector about his activities, although this does not lead to any official intervention. The 'masters of our academic state' (2.5) play a more prominent, although essentially comic, part in Robert Greene's *Friar Bacon and Friar Bungay* (? 1589–90). The scholar, like the playwright and the actor, could enjoy a privileged marginality within Renaissance societies and thus became a figure around whom social anxieties as well as aspirations gathered. Faustus is a particular kind of masterless man. He finds his master when he signs the contract with Lucifer.

Most of Marlowe's spectators believed not just in witchcraft but, more specifically, that Lucifer sought out solitary, masterless people to do his work for him. There is thus a very general similarity between a learned magus like Faustus and the women who were accused of practising more popular forms of magic. Keith Thomas shows in *Religion and the Decline of Magic* (1973) that the majority of convicted witches were poor women who were confined to the margins of society. Their marginality was often literal and geographical, as indeed it is represented as being in Shakespeare's *Macbeth* (1606). It was also political since they were associated with unsuccessful attempts to revive old habits of what Thomas calls 'neighbourliness' (p. 660) to combat an increasing emphasis on forms of possessive individualism. The refusal of chestnuts leads to retaliation in *Macbeth* and *The Witch of Edmonton* (1621), by Dekker and others, shows Elizabeth Sawyer being refused permission to gather firewood. Witchcraft trials tell the same story. Joan Cunny, who was hanged at Chelmsford in 1589, confessed that she had employed witchcraft against a neighbour who had refused her a drink. Feelings of guilt often prompted the prosperous to lay the natural evils that befell them at the doors of solitary and poverty-stricken homes. A desire for explanations in an unpredictable environment also led to the construction of the witch as a particularly malicious form of alien stranger. Marginality was usually defined in physical, or bodily, terms as well. Elizabeth Sawyer, who was based upon a convicted witch of the same name, claims that she is victimised because of her deformed and grotesque body, which is 'like a bow buckl'd and bent together' (2.1.4). The evidence indicates that convictions for witchcraft were particularly high in the 1580s and 1590s, which were also decades associated with the increased demonisation of other marginalised groups such as Catholics, Puritans and Jews.

The witch was also pursued and persecuted because she was seen as inhabiting the margins, or liberties, of patriarchy. This did not generally mean, as it often did in continental Europe, that she was represented as being sexually uncontrollable to the point where only Lucifer himself was able to satisfy her 'unnatural' desires. It tended to mean that she was endowed with 'unwoman-ly', or masculine, characteristics. She may have been a marginal figure and yet she was credited with the power to undermine the central institutions of a community. She became a target for male anxieties about powerful women who evaded their surveillance and control. Women who were held to be 'scolds' were sometimes confined and displayed, like plague victims, in cages. Witches were physically tortured even before they reached the scaffold. One of the popular remedies against witchcraft was to draw the blood of the witch by scratching her 'above the breath', in other words on the face. Scolds and witches were punished because they were seen as being masterless and therefore potentially masterful. Their mouths had to be stopped because they were held to be like common sewers.

Writers such as Reginald Scot in *The Discoverie of Witchcraft* (1584) advanced sceptical arguments against belief in witchcraft and pacts with Lucifer. He suggests that the chief fault of those convicted for witchcraft was often that they were either scolds or cozeners. He relates the widespread acceptance of witchcraft to the increasing effeminacy of society, declaring that warriors like the Scythians were untroubled by evil spirits. His was nevertheless a minority opinion on both Scythians and witches. Thomas produces evidence, such as accounts of sightings of Lucifer, to support the view that, for the majority, 'the literal reality of demons seemed a fundamental article of faith' (p. 567) in the sixteenth century. This is why it is dangerous to read the stories of real devils appearing during a performance of *Doctor Faustus* as being just theatrical hype and to underestimate more generally the ways in which the play might have terrified spectators. Although there are important differences between the magus and the witch, it is nevertheless possible to see them both as masterless people who were held to threaten society.

Some critics, while not necessarily rejecting the idea of a frightening play, suggest that it may also be more self-consciously playful in its representation of the Devils. Such arguments depend upon distinctions between different versions of Hell. Faustus's disputes with Mephostophilis, whom he raises in the 'solitary grove', can present Hell as a state of mind:

Faustus	How comes it then that thou art out of hell?
Mephostophilis	Why, this is hell, nor am I out of it.
	Think'st thou that I who saw the face of God
	And tasted the eternal joys of heaven,

Am not tormented with ten thousand hells
In being depriv'd of everlasting bliss?

(1.3. 75–80)

Hell is defined here in terms of the mental torment caused by the
absence of God. Faustus responds to this in the same way as
Mortimer reacts to Isabella's speeches in *Edward II*. He declares
that Mephostophilis is being too 'passionate' (1.3.83) and ought to
acquire some 'manly fortitude' (1.3.85). There are other moments
in these dialogues, or disputes, when Hell is seen as being a
physical location, under the heavens, where the inhabitants are
physically tortured. This is what Philip Stubbes and others describe
as a material Hell populated with ugly, or 'ugglesome', devils. It
has been suggested that both these versions of Hell can be
associated with distinctive theatrical styles. The representation of
the Hell of mental torment and absence, it is argued, is dependent
on soliloquies and other theatrical devices that are identifiably
Elizabethan. The representation of the Hell of physical torment,
by contrast, requires the self-conscious recreation of medieval
theatrical styles. The play's playfulness can then be seen as taking
the form of a series of dramatic parodies which render Lucifer and
the Devils as much figures of fun as of terror.

Lucifer is described in *A Homily against Disobedience and
Wilful Rebellion* (1571) as being 'the grand Captain and father of
all rebels' (A2). He and some of his followers form an on-stage
audience for Faustus's incantations. He shares, with the theatre
audience, the secrets of the 'solitary grove'. Yet he also shares the
concerns of the Renaissance prince. He may be an outcast who
stands for rebellion against legally constituted authority and yet he
demands that Faustus should draft a legal document, or 'deed of
gift' (2.1.35), specifying the details of their contract. Faustus rails
against the drudgery of law and yet his allegiance to Lucifer does
not provide the escape that he desires. Lucifer is the 'father of all
rebels', but he is also the 'Prince of the East' (2.1.105) who legally
binds his subjects to him to prevent them from rebelling. Faustus's
rejection of the law ultimately takes a highly legalistic form.

The legal document that Faustus writes with his blood has no
status according to Christian interpretations because he does not
own, and therefore is unable to sell, his soul. It also quickly

becomes apparent that Mephostophilis is quite prepared to insert qualifications into the document after it has been signed. He refuses to find Faustus a wife because to do so would be to lend support to Christian ceremonies. He chooses not to reveal all his knowledge about the creation of the world. Faustus, who wanted to escape from the aridity of disputes as well as from the drudgery of the law, finds himself reduced to arguing 'freshmen's suppositions' (2.2.55) with Mephostophilis. The book that he is given appears to have been heavily censored. Lucifer censors knowledge to protect his kingdom. Faustus's bid for freedom is contained by his new master, who is called Lucifer but whose tactics bear a close resemblance to those of the Renaissance prince. The escape from the 'quiet house' to the 'solitary grove' leads to the imposition of some of the very restrictions it was designed to remove. This may be Faustus's tragedy.

7.3 Such Conceits as Clownage Keeps in Pay

The short, sharp Prologue to the first part of *Tamburlaine* has often been read as providing support for the view that Marlowe was hostile towards 'such conceits as clownage keeps in pay' (1.2). His Prologues should not, however, be read so literally. This one is after all followed immediately by scenes of 'clownage' involving Mycetes. Although Elizabethan plays were certainly collectively authored, it is still a modern prejudice to claim that Marlowe's voice is always absent from comic scenes.

Faustus's servant, Wagner, resembles his master in being able to convince himself that he excels in dispute. He is questioned about Faustus's movements by two Scholars when he is fetching some wine. Their haughty greeting – 'How now, sirrah, where's thy master?' (1.2.4) – encourages him to turn the scholastic tables:

Yet if you were not dunces, you would never ask me such a question. For is he not *corpus naturale*? And is not that *mobile*? Then wherefore should you ask me such a question? . . . Thus, having triumphed over you, I will set my countenance like a precisian, and begin to speak thus: Truly, my dear brethren, my master is within at dinner with Valdes and Cornelius, as this

wine, if it could speak, would inform your worships. And so the
Lord bless you, preserve you and keep you, my dear brethren.

(1.2.12–22)

The scene holds up a comic mirror to Faustus's dispute about
forms of knowledge. The two Scholars may have been dressed in
gowns and ruffs as badges of their superior status and yet they are
unable to make a simple deduction. If Wagner is returning home
with some wine, then it should be obvious that Faustus dines at
home. The exchange offers a comic version of a university dispute,
in which Wagner turns the swords of the Scholars against them.
Faustus may resemble these Scholars as he too, despite all his
learning, is reluctant to see the obvious. He quotes a passage from
the Bible which decrees 'everlasting death' to sinners without
looking to see what is promised to them if they repent. It is only
much later that the spectators learn that Mephostophilis may have
intervened to prevent him from reading about repentance. This
admission makes Faustus less of a tragic figure by denying him
real choice. Wagner mocks Puritan, or 'precisian', modes of
address with his 'Truly, my dear brethren' and mimics the blessing.
He plays a blasphemous version of the 'bashful puritan'.

Wagner may triumph over the Scholars, although he in turn
finds himself upstaged by Robin, the clown. He loftily attempts to
recruit Robin into his service:

Wagner   Come hither, sirrah boy.
Robin   Boy? O disgrace to my person! Zounds, boy in your
           face! You have seen many boys with such pickadevants,
           I am sure.

(1.4.1–3)

Wagner is the beardless boy whereas Robin, if not a comic old
man, is at least much older than him. This helps to explain why
Robin is able to establish himself as the dominant partner in the
double act. Wagner tries to bribe this masterless man into service
with the prospect of food, but is only feeding the more established
comedian his punchlines:

Wagner   I know the villain's out of service and so hungry that I

know he would give his soul to the devil for a shoulder of
mutton, though it were blood-raw.

Robin   Not so neither. I had need to have it well roasted, and
good sauce to it, if I pay so dear, I can tell you.
(1.4.6–10)

Faustus sells his soul to Lucifer so that he can feed both an
intellectual and a sensual appetite. Robin believes that, if he is
going to be well roasted in Hell, then he ought to strike the best
bargain possible. This saucy fellow may be more perceptive than
the learned Faustus. Wagner has to resort to tempting him with
new clothes and a purse of guilders. He accepts the money and yet,
as soon as he realises that this means that Lucifer might fetch him,
tries to break the contract by returning the money. The comedians
juggle the purse of guilders between them. Robin waits fearlessly
for the appearance of the Devils and cracks grotesque jokes about
them: 'Belcher? And Belcher come here, I'll belch him! I am not
afraid of a devil' (1.4.29–30). He nevertheless '*runs up and down
crying*', according to the stage directions, as soon as the Devils
appear. Perhaps he tries to escape through the audience and is
pushed back. The comedy is primarily visual with the frightened
Robin making a number of acrobatic falls and leaps. Spectators
may share his fear, while laughing at his antics. It is fear rather
than material rewards that persuade him to accept Wagner as his
master. They exit with Robin, still dressed in rags, offering an
exaggerated parody of an attentive servant following at his new
master's heels. Perhaps it is also fear that prevents Faustus from
terminating his contract. Perhaps Lucifer expects him to be a very
deferential servant.

Wagner tries to imitate Faustus and the pattern repeats itself
when Robin tries to imitate Wagner. Robin's mastery of his new
master's conjuring skills is handicapped by the fact that he is
almost illiterate. He steals a book and yet has difficulty making
sense of it as written English and Latin are both foreign languages
to him:

Robin   *A per se a, t.h.e. the: o per se o, deny orgon, gorgon.* Keep
further from me, O thou illiterate and unlearned hostler.

Dick   'Snails, what hast thou got there? A book? Why, thou
           can't not tell ne're a word on't.

                                                      (2.3.6–10)

Robin may not be able to read, but Dick appears to have some
difficulty recognising a book for what it is. The Clown in Shakespeare's *Romeo and Juliet* (?1591–6) has similar problems with
the written word. He is unable to read the names of the guests
whom Capulet wants to be invited to the masked ball. Faustus is
highly literate and yet is still unable to read certain passages.
Although Robin makes a magic circle, his inability to read the
incantation means that he is unable to frighten Dick by raising
devils. So they set off for the tavern believing that they have the
power to magic away the bill. Perhaps they are like Faustus in that
they propose to surfeit themselves while remaining unconcerned
about how the reckoning might be exacted.

Robin's attempts at conjuring appear once again to have been
unsuccessful since he and Dick flee from the tavern with a stolen
cup. They are pursued by the Vintner. They juggle the cup
between themselves, probably in much the same way that the
guilders had been passed to and fro earlier on, and then hide it
from the Vintner. It should not be hidden from the audience.
Elizabethan clowns had different specialities. Will Kemp, who
belonged to the Lord Chamberlain's Men in the 1590s, was famous
for dancing jigs. The clown who created the part of Robin seems to
have been an experienced juggler. Perhaps this is all that Faustus
becomes as a result of this contract with Lucifer.

Robin's third attempt at employing magic is, much to his own
surprise and that of many spectators, remarkably successful. He
terrifies the Vintner by raising a very petulant Mephostophilis. He
himself had stumbled and tumbled about the stage when Wagner
had raised Devils. This time he stands his ground and allows the
great Mephostophilis to feed him his lines. Dick is transformed
into an ape and Robin is quick to spot the commercial possibilities
of a new double act: 'O brave, an ape! I pray sir, let me have the
carrying of him about to show some tricks' (3.3.38–9). Dogs were
used to carry apes on their backs in the bear-baiting arenas such as
Paris Gardens that were situated close to the public theatres.
Mephostophilis's revenge on the clowns rebounds comically on
him since he unwittingly provides them with a new career.

The comic scenes form an integral part of the play because they question Faustus's actions. They may contain blasphemy, for instance when Wagner mocks the blessing, and yet they still manage to suggest orthodox responses to Faustus's contract with Lucifer.

7.4 Theatres of Hell

Theatre and theatricality are associated with Hell throughout the play. Faustus's house, and the theatrical house itself, are quiet until the arrival of the Devils. Such an association was commonplace in Elizabethan propaganda against the public theatres. They are denigrated as enchanted places, where unsuspecting spectators ran the very real risk of being charmed and bewitched. This play, like the *Tamburlaine* plays and *Edward II*, confirms nightmares about the theatre and yet it too does so in such an emphatic and outrageous way as to challenge the propaganda.

Mephostophilis appears first of all as an actor. He enters the 'solitary grove' in the shape of a dragon, but is ordered by Faustus to wear another costume:

> I charge thee to return and change thy shape,
> Thou art too ugly to attend on me.
> Go, and return an old Franciscan friar,
> That holy shape becomes a devil best.
>
> (1.3.23–6)

Faustus plays the playwright, cuing entrances and exits as well as ordering costume changes, whereas Mephostophilis appears to be the obedient actor. Their subsequent dialogue nevertheless reveals that Faustus's theatrical control is an illusion, or shadow. Mephostophilis is not the slave of Faustus's magical script, but has come of his 'own accord' (1.3.44). He turns out to be a playwright who stages shows so that Faustus himself will be more pliant. Perhaps he plays Gaveston to Faustus's Edward. Faustus has second thoughts immediately after signing the contract with Lucifer, so Mephostophilis cues in some entertainment to 'delight his mind' (2.1.82). He is given a crown. When he asks for a wife the playwright stages another distracting show: 'I'll fetch thee a wife in the devil's name' (2.2.143–4). The part is played, according to the stage directions, by '*a* Devil *dressed like a woman*'. Just as the play as a whole is so open about connections between theatricality and Hell, so it flaunts the practices of cross-dressing. It is a way of taunting the propagandists.

Faustus rejects the parts of logician, doctor, lawyer and priest in the opening scene in favour of writing a script over which he has more control. He ends up playing the part of a spectator for Mephostophilis's plays. This theme is continued with the Pageant of the Seven Deadly Sins. Faustus responds to the words of the Good Angel by calling on Christ to forgive him. He is, once again, in danger of departing from the script that has been written for him. Lucifer, Belzebub and Mephostophilis make a dramatic entrance. Lucifer, like Ferneze in *The Jew of Malta*, delivers a short, sharp monologue of power:

> Christ cannot save thy soul, for he is just;
> There's none but I have interest in the same.
>
> (2.2.85–6)

He goes on to demand that Faustus keeps the promises encoded in the legal contract, which assumes the status of Ferneze's decrees. He receives an assurance that the rebel does not intend to stage a rebellion against him:

Lucifer   So shalt thou show thyself an obedient servant,
          And we will highly gratify thee for it.
Belzebub Faustus, we are come from hell in person to show thee
          some pastime. Sit down and thou shalt behold the
          Seven Deadly Sins appear to thee in their own proper
          shapes and likeness.
Faustus   That sight will be as pleasant to me as Paradise was to
          Adam the first day of his creation.
Lucifer   Talk not of Paradise or Creation, but mark the show.
          Go, Mephostophilis, fetch them in.

> (2.2.100–8)

Lucifer's terrible appearance may have frightened Elizabethan audiences and yet his monologue of power would have been instantly recognisable as the language of the prince. It may be that the mechanics of his system of social control, involving total obedience followed by limited gratification, would also have been familiar. Lucifer is both a demon from another world and a recognisably Renaissance prince who self-consciously employs spectacle and display to consolidate his power. He can be seen as another of Marlowe's Machiavellian rulers.

Faustus is allowed to become an actor in, as well as a spectator of, the Pageant of the Seven Deadly Sins. He is invited to question each of the Sins. When his allegiances to Hell are thought to be secure enough, he can indulge himself as a performer. He arrives in Rome with Mephostophilis and desires a new part to be written for him:

> Then in this show let me an actor be,
> That this proud Pope may Faustus' cunning see. (3.1.76–7)

Mephostophilis asks him to continue to play the part of a spectator before choosing the part that he wants to act. The play that Faustus watches involves the ritual humiliation of Bruno by the Pope. Bruno, who is held to be a Protestant heretic, is in chains and has to kneel down so that the Pope can climb up on his back to ascend to 'Saint Peter's chair' (3.1.98). The Pope plays Tamburlaine to Bruno's Bajazeth. The scene employs, as the stage directions indicate, the full ceremonial power of the Catholic Church to reinforce the messages of this particular sight of power:

> *Enter the* Cardinals *and* Bishops, *some bearing crosiers, some the pillars*; Monks *and* Friars *singing their procession.*

Actors play priests. Power is visualised through processions, or passages, across the stage. More specifically, the ceremonial procession derives its power from being allowed to precede the grotesque procession of the chained Bruno.

Faustus and Mephostophilis disrupt this display of power by freeing Bruno and then dressing up as cardinals. They too are actors who play priests. The theatre of misrule is characterised, as it is in *The Jew of Malta*, by the speed of its improvisations. Faustus ultimately gains theatrical rather than intellectual pleasure from his contract with Lucifer. He is allowed to cause further disruption by moving unseen around the Papal banquet snatching food, wine and other items away from the participants. It is a banquet of the senses which reveals that the Pope and his court commit many of the Deadly Sins. Perhaps the parts were played by the same actors on the Elizabethan stage. Such a representation fits in with Protestant versions of the Pope as anti-Christ. Spectators are, once again, being placed in ambiguous positions. They are asked to condemn Faustus for his pact with Lucifer at the same time as they are encouraged to applaud him for playing practical jokes on a national enemy. Bad angels, like Mephostophilis, have been recruited to fight on the side of the good angels against another set of bad angels. Some of the ambiguities that attach themselves to Tamburlaine's role as the 'Scourge of God' are present here. Faustus employs demonic means to achieve what would have been seen as a worthy end. Reginald Scot suggests that there is no difference between the rites and rituals of the Catholic Church and those employed by magicians. They are both seen as being blasphemous and fraudulent. Marlowe, by contrast, shows the triumph of magic over Catholic spells such as the ritual cursing by bell, book and candle. Burghley refers in *The Execution of Justice in England* to the way in which Elizabeth herself was cursed, or excommunicated, by the Pope. Faustus and Mephostophilis are therefore, disconcertingly, allowed to speak for England when they ridicule the Pope's curses.

Faustus becomes a professional entertainer, or playwright, who stages shows for emperors and dukes. He is welcomed to the Court of Charles the Fifth where, with Mephostophilis's aid, he stages classical dumb shows for a coterie audience. The play very self-consciously stages another play within itself before an on-stage audience. The weaknesses as well as the strengths of the playwright are explored. Faustus can raise the shapes of Alexander and his paramour and yet there is also something unsettling and unsatisfactory about this show: 'these are but shadows, not substantial' (4.1.99). The Emperor himself may be convinced by the life-like qualities of Faustus's representations, although other members of the on-stage audience are not nearly so receptive. The patrician Benvolio starts off by heckling Faustus, declaring that he 'looks as like a conjurer as the Pope to a costermonger' (4.1.72) and then falls asleep. He is turned into a spectacle for threatening to disrupt the spectacle.

Faustus has the power either to please or to coerce his audience and yet the limitations of this power are also revealed. The festive celebration of a demonic theatricality, which characterises the scenes set in Rome, is increasingly accompanied by a more pessimistic awareness of the playwright's powerlessness. Theatre and theatricality produce a complicated mixture of enchantment and disenchantment. Faustus's earlier fantasies of imperial conquest and political influence have not materialised. He is still dependent upon patronage. His shows do not change the world, but merely allow himself and others to pass the time within it. This would have passed away, although perhaps not so pleasurably. The characters that he creates are dumb and he commands his audience to view them in 'dumb silence' (4.1.93). Theatricality is represented as both filling empty spaces and being an empty space itself.

Benvolio seeks revenge by planning to ambush and kill the 'peasant' (4.2.35) Faustus in a 'grove' (4.2.16). His indifference and then hostility towards a successful, but basely-born, playwright can be located within Elizabethan polemics against the theatre. Faustus is, however, indestructible because of the events that occurred in another grove. He has his head cut off only for it to be revealed to be a false one. The same theatrical trick, which is very effective when seen for the first time, is used in the morality play *Mankind* (?1460–5) and probably had its origins in Mummers' plays. It is entirely appropriate that an arrogant critic of the theatre should be defeated through the use of such an old theatrical gag. Faustus may escape death on this occasion, but the way in which Benvolio and his accomplices gloat over the task of dismembering his apparently lifeless body anticipates the hour of his death. This also happens when the Horse-Courser pulls off what turns out to be a false leg.

Faustus stages another show, this time to pass the time for the Duke and Duchess of Vanholt. He erects an 'enchanted castle in the air' (4.6.2–3) for the Duke and fetches a bunch of grapes for the Duchess. There is, once again, a sense of emptiness about his theatrical achievements. A question is also being raised about how far all of his patrons share in the guilt of his pact with Lucifer. They derive pleasure from his demonic skills and yet do not have to suffer any of the accompanying mental and physical torture. It is a question that is also being posed to the spectators in the theatre. Are those who surfeited themselves on the spectacle of Faustus and Mephostophilis ridiculing the Pope guilty of forming their own pact with Lucifer? The performance at Vanholt is interrupted by the arrival of the Horse-Courser, Robin, Dick and other members of the tavern world. They lurch in to accuse Faustus of being a fraud. This time it is plebeians rather than patricians who exhibit hostility towards the playwright. Faustus stages another of his dumb shows for the 'merriment' (4.6.45) of his noble patrons. He strikes the drunken hecklers dumb one after the other. The Duke and Duchess collude in this use of his demonic powers: 'His artful sport drives all sad thoughts away' (4.6.108). They are on-stage spectators who are in the privileged position of being able to enjoy the theatre of Hell without being made to suffer for it. They can surfeit themselves with forbidden fruit and yet not bother about the reckoning. The theatre spectators are in the same position. They too have been entertained by the 'artful sport' which Faustus, with Mephostophilis's aid, has provided for them. They are nevertheless going to be asked to march away applauding his death.

7.5 The Hour of Faustus's Death

Faustus returns home for the final act in Lucifer's play. He gives no outward sign of repentance. Wagner reports that his master continues to 'banquet and carouse and swill' (5.1.6) with the students. Jerzy Grotowski's 1963 production for the Polish Laboratory Theatre began with this banquet and then allowed Faustus to recall the events leading up to it. Faustus indulges the students with after-dinner magic displays such as the raising of the spirit of Helen of Troy. It is a dumb show that strikes the students momentarily dumb with admiration for Helen. They are spectators whose voyeuristic desires are gratified by Faustus's demonic theatrical powers. Perhaps they are also accomplices in the pact with Lucifer, despite the fact that they appear to be surprised and shocked when they learn about it later on.

Faustus is chided by the Good Angel at various points during the play, although this voice is always in dialogue with that of the Bad Angel. These characters have their origins in earlier plays such as *The Castle of Perseverance* (?1410–25). The Old Man who enters immediately after the banquet offers a more sustained version of the Good Angel's case against Faustus. He corrects Faustus's earlier interpretation of the Bible by indicating that all sinners have opportunities for repentance:

> Though thou hast now offended like a man,
> Do not persever in it like a devil.
> Yet, yet, thou hast an amiable soul,
> If sin by custom grow not into nature:
> Then, Faustus, will repentance come too late,
> Then thou art banish'd from the sight of heaven;
> No mortal can express the pains of hell. (5.1.39–45)

This and his subsequent speeches force Faustus, momentarily, to regret his actions. His despair is nevertheless mocked by Mephostophilis, who continues to demand total obedience:

> Thou traitor, Faustus, I arrest thy soul
> For disobedience to my sovereign Lord.
> Revolt, or I'll in piecemeal tear thy flesh. (5.1.72–4)

The rebel is not allowed to revolt against 'the father of all rebels'. Faustus re-affirms his allegiance to the 'Prince of the East' and asks for the Old Man to be punished. Mephostophilis's answer appears to underline the truth of the Old Man's words as he claims that he has little power over those with strong 'faith' (5.1.85). A similar moment occurs in *The Witch of Edmonton* when Dog confesses that he only has power to touch those who are already disposed to curse and swear against God. Faustus appears to receive confirmation that the only power that the Devils have over the human soul is that which is given to them.

Faustus does not, however, hear this revealing remark. He is too concerned to get Mephostophilis to stage yet another show to delight and distract his senses:

> One thing, good servant, let me crave of thee,
> To glut the longing of my heart's desire,
> That I may have unto my paramour
> That heavenly Helen which I saw of late, . . . (5.1.88–91)

Faustus, like the students, is bewitched by Helen's beauty:

> Was this the face that launch'd a thousand ships,
> And burnt the topless towers of Ilium?
> Sweet Helen, make me immortal with a kiss:
> Her lips suck forth my soul, see where it flies. (5.1.97–100)

The Old Man has no time for Faustus's poetic responses:

> Accursed Faustus, miserable man,
> That from thy soul exclud'st the grace of heaven,
> And fliest the throne of his tribunal seat. (5.1.117–20)

Some critics argue that the Old Man is pronouncing an eternal death sentence here because Faustus intends to make love to an evil spirit, which has assumed the pleasing shape of Helen. Others suggest that Faustus still has an opportunity to repent and yet either decides, or is forced, not to do so. This means that the conventional structure of the morality play, in which ignorance produces a fall that nevertheless leads to redemption, is being disrupted. One of the problems for the spectators during these exchanges is that Faustus has the most memorable lines. The Old Man may have the kind of choric authority that was granted to characters like Good Counsel in earlier drama and yet, rhetorically, he is eminently forgettable. As already noted, he claims that 'No mortal can express the pains of hell'. Elizabethan spectators who were familiar with the plague pits, scaffolds and prisons might have disagreed with him. He also neatly sidesteps the real problem, which is how to express the pleasures of Heaven. He is unable to do this, certainly to Faustus's satisfaction, and so his voice is both granted and denied authority. Faustus's address to Helen is more memorable than either the Old Man's speeches or Mephostophilis's admission of impotence. It is a problem that is only compounded by the eloquence of Faustus's final soliloquy. The gods appear to be silent in the *Tamburlaine* plays. The voice of religious orthodoxy can certainly be heard in *Doctor Faustus*, although here it lacks the rhetorical power of the competing voice.

The hour of Faustus's death is another theatrical event that is self-consciously staged before on-stage spectators. Lucifer and his

followers enter and process to the gallery to watch this spectacle of
suffering:

> Thus from infernal Dis do we ascend
> To view the subjects of our monarchy,
> Those souls which sin seals the black sons of hell,
> 'Mong which as chief, Faustus, we come to thee,
> Bringing with us lasting damnation
> To wait upon thy soul; the time is come
> Which makes it forfeit. (5.2.1–7)

They may appear to be grotesque and yet Lucifer's language – 'To
view the subjects of our monarchy' – is that of the Renaissance
prince. The Devils also take up the positions that were usually
reserved, if not for the monarch, then for members of the Privy
Council and other dignitaries at public executions. Marlowe's
stage becomes, once again, a scaffold. Lucifer and his attendants
witness Faustus taking his leave of the Scholars. The Second
Scholar pleads with Faustus to 'look up to heaven, and remember
God's mercy is infinite' (5.2.37–8). The gallery, or Heaven of the
stage, is however already occupied by Lucifer. Another prologue
to the main event is provided by the final appearance of the Good
and Bad Angels. The Good Angel reminds Faustus of the eternal
world that he has lost, although faces the same problem that
confronted the Old Man. The pleasures of Heaven must ultimately
remain 'unspeakable' (5.2.100). Perhaps the heavenly throne that
descends at this point conveys a more positive message about
them. The Bad Angel does a much better job expressing the pains
of Hell:

> Now, Faustus, let thine eyes with horror stare
> Into that vast perpetual torture-house.
> There are the furies tossing damned souls
> On burning forks; there bodies boil in lead;
> There are live quarters broiling on the coals
> That ne'er can die; . . . (5.2.109–14)

Faustus will die on the scaffold only to suffer thousands of deaths
afterwards. This was an orthodox Elizabethan attitude towards

punishment and, as such, would have been supported by Mr Boyes. It is, however, delivered here by a Bad Angel. Faustus is, according to Mephostophilis, being punished for his pursuit of pleasure: 'Fools that will laugh on earth, must weep in hell' (5.2.91). Mephostophilis the entertainer now assumes the puritanical shapes of Philip Gawdy and Thomas Beard. The theatre spectators are, yet again, placed in a difficult position. Their love of pleasure has brought them to the playhouse in the first place. The condemned man on the scaffold has staged a riot of spectacle and carnivalesque excess for their delight. They are now being asked to approve of his execution. Matters are complicated still further by the fact that the on-stage audience consists of Lucifer and his followers. Spectators who applaud Faustus's punishment may be in danger of forming their own pact with Lucifer because they both want the same thing.

Faustus is no longer the playwright who either charms, or coerces, his audiences. His power has been an illusion, or shadow. He is an actor who is condemned to play the part that has been written for him in the theatre of Hell. He must deliver his dying speech from the scaffold and then meet his executioners. He nevertheless continues to rebel by imagining that he can control time:

> Stand still, you ever-moving spheres of heaven,
> That time may cease and midnight never come.
> Fair nature's eye, rise, rise again, and make
> Perpetual day; or let this hour be but
> A year, a month, a week, a natural day,
> That Faustus may repent and save his soul. (5.2.129–34)

He appears to realise the futility of this attempt to postpone both the hour of his death and his repentance:

> O I'll leap up to my God! Who pulls me down?
> See, see, where Christ's blood streams in the firmament!
> One drop would save my soul, half a drop. Ah, my Christ!
> Rend not my heart for naming of my Christ! (5.2.138–41)

His language leaps, or soars, and in some productions this movement is accompanied by a physical attempt to escape from

the confines of the stage. He tries to ascend and then, when he
starts to contemplate the vengeful God of the Old Testament,
looks for a way of disappearing beneath the stage:

> Mountains and hills, come, come, and fall on me,
> And hide me from the heavy wrath of God.
> No, no!
> Then will I headlong run into the earth.
> Earth, gape! O no, it will not harbour me. (5.2.146–50)

There is no hiding place. He remains trapped on the stage, much
to the delight of the on-stage audience. The prologue to his
punishment for the pursuit of pleasure provides pleasure for his
pursuers.

Barabas and Edward are executed in front of the theatre
audience. The text is not so clear about the location for Faustus's
first death. It probably takes place beneath the stage, to the
accompaniment of 'fearful shrieks and cries' (5.3.4). His 'mangl'd
limbs' (5.3.17) are then thrown back up onto the stage through the
trap-door that represents the mouth of Hell. They are discovered
the next day by the Scholars:

> 2 *Scholar* Oh help us, heaven! See, here are Faustus' limbs,
> All torn asunder by the hand of death. (5.3.6–7)

The stage continues to resemble the scaffold, although the Scholars break with convention by declaring their intention to bury the
dismembered body. The final Chorus is nevertheless more orthodox:

> Faustus is gone: regard his hellish fall,
> Whose fiendful fortune may exhort the wise
> Only to wonder at unlawful things,
> Whose deepness doth entice such forward wits
> To practise more than heavenly power permits. (4–8)

The play ends, as it began, with a homily against disobedience and
wilful rebellion. It is, however, 'the grand Captain and father of all
rebels' who stages Faustus's execution.

Frances Yates suggests in *The Occult Philosophy in the Elizabethan Age* (1983) that this concluding homily contains the 'moral' (p.119) of the play. This allows her to claim that *Doctor Faustus* is part of the late sixteenth-century movement against Renaissance ideas. She also situates *The Jew of Malta* within the same context. Marlowe's resolutions should not, however, be read so literally. They may offer an answer to conflicts and yet this is no guarantee that they themselves will not be open to conflicting interpretations. Orthodox voices are certainly heard throughout *Doctor Faustus*. Both the Good Angel and the Old Man put the Christian case against Faustus's actions. There are also disconcerting moments when Mephostophilis, who has seen the 'face of God', joins the chorus of disapproval. The comic scenes in the earlier part of the play raise a series of potentially damning questions about Faustus's contract with Lucifer, even though they can be seen as representing a blasphemous critique of blasphemy. The increasing emptiness of Faustus's theatricality also casts a dark shadow over the contract. The play does not, however, confine itself to a straightforward homily on Faustus's 'hellish fall'. He has the most memorable lines. His theatricality, particularly during the scenes in Rome, is capable of filling empty spaces. He provides the spectators on this occasion with highly orthodox pleasures. Here and elsewhere, the categories that are taken as read by the resolution are unsettled. It is, for instance, difficult to maintain the sharp distinction between the lawful and the 'unlawful' if Lucifer is seen as a Renaissance prince who legally binds his subjects to him to prevent them from rebelling. Lucifer and his followers gloat over Faustus's execution. So too does the Chorus who delivers the resolution. Heaven and Hell appear to be on the same side. The Chorus, like the Old Man and the Good Angel, has no solution to the problem of how to describe the pleasures of Heaven. He just maintains that there are 'things' which are not permitted by 'heavenly power'. Lucifer and Mephostophilis control their own kingdom along the same lines. They actively prevent Faustus from acquiring any knowledge that might threaten their power. The resolution needs to be seen as continuing rather than settling the debates and disputes that run throughout the play.

Selected Bibliography

As mentioned at the beginning of the book, some students might wish to go straight to the third section of the bibliography. They will find there a relatively short list of books and articles on Marlowe's plays and the Elizabethan theatre. Those that have been starred are the ones that I consider to be particularly useful. The first section identifies the texts that have been used and therefore fills in some of the gaps created by the absence of footnotes. Most titles have been abbreviated and the dates beside plays refer to first performances rather than publication. The second section indicates some of the secondary sources that have been used in the reconstruction of Elizabethan society. It will, hopefully, help students who want to do their own contextual work on Marlowe's plays.

Texts

Anon. *The Castle of Perseverance,* Peter Happe (ed.), *Four Morality Plays* (? 1410–25, Penguin Books, Harmondsworth, 1979).
——*The Fall of Lucifer,* R. M. Lumiansky and David Mills (eds), *The Chester Mystery Cycle* (?1467–1488, Oxford University Press, 1974).

—— *The Historie of the Damnable Life and Deserved Death of Doctor John Faustus* (1592; reprinted by University of Notre Dame Press, Notre Dame, 1963).

—— *A Homily against Disobedience and Wilful Rebellion* (Richard Jugge and John Cawood, London, 1571).

—— *Mankind*, Glynne Wickham (ed.), *English Moral Interludes* (? 1460–5, Dent, London, 1976).

—— *A True and Plain Declaration of the Horrible Treasons, Practised by William Parry the Traitor, against the Queenes Majesty ...* (Christopher Barker, London, 1585).

Baldwin, William et al *The Mirror for Magistrates* (1559–87; reprinted by Barnes and Noble, New York, 1960).

Beard, Thomas *The Theatre of God's Judgements* (Adam Islip, London, 1597).

Brecht, Bertolt *The Life of Edward II of England*, John Willett and Ralph Mannheim (eds), *Collected Plays*, 8 vols, I (1924, Eyre Methuen, London, 1980).

Camden, William *Annales: The True and Royal History of the Famous Empress Elizabeth Queen of England* (Benjamin Fisher, London, 1625).

Cecil, William Lord Burghley *The Execution of Justice in England* (1583; reprinted by Cornell University Press, Ithaca, 1965).

Cobbett, William (ed.) *Cobbett's Complete Collection of State Trials and Proceedings for High Treason*, 33 vols, I (R. Bagshaw, London, 1809 and subsequently).

Cosin, Richard *Conspiracy for a Pretended Reformation ... A Treatise Discovering the late Designments and Courses held for Advancement thereof, by William Hacket, Yeoman, Edmund Coppinger, and Henry Arthington* (Deputies of C. Barker, London, 1592).

Cunny, Joan *The Arraignment of Execution of Joan Cunny of Stisted in the County of Essex* (1589; reprinted in Barbara Rosen (ed.), *Witchcraft* (Edward Arnold, London, 1969).

Dasent, John Roche (ed.) *Acts of the Privy Council of England*, vols 14–24 (1901, Kraus Reprint, Nendelm/Liechtenstein, 1974).

Dekker, Thomas *Dekker His Dreame* (Nicholas Okes, London, 1620).

—— *Newes from Hell* (Ralph Blower, London, 1606).

—— *The Seven Deadly Sins of London* (1606; reprinted by

Benjamin Blom, New York, 1966).

—— *Villanies Discovered by Lanthorne and Candelight* (John Busby, London, 1616).

——*The Witch of Edmonton* (1621, Methuen, London, 1983). Written in collaboration with Thomas Middleton and William Rowley.

—— *The Wonderful Year 1603 wherein is shown the Picture of London lying Sick of the Plague* (Thomas Creede, London, 1603).

D'Ewes, Sir Simonds (ed.) *A Compleat Journal of the Votes, Speeches and Debates both of the House of Lords and House of Commons throughout the Reign of Queen Elizabeth of Glorious Memory* (Jonathan Robinson, London, 1708).

Elizabeth I, Queen *The True Copy of a Letter from the Queenes Majesty to the Lord Mayor and his Brethren* (Christopher Barker, London, 1586).

Foxe, John *Actes and Monuments* (1563 and subsequently; reprinted in 8 vols by Seeley and Burnside, London, 1837–41).

Gawdy, Philip I. H. Jeayes (ed.), *Letters of Philip Gawdy of West Harling, Norfolk, and of London, to various Members of his Family 1579–1616* (J. B. Nichols and Sons, London, 1906).

Gentillet, Innocent C. Edward Rathe (ed.), *Anti-Machiavel; Edition de 1576* (Librairie Droz, Geneva, 1968).

Gerard, John *John Gerard: The Autobiography of a Hunted Priest*, Philip Caraman (trans.), (Longman, London 1951).

Gilbert, Sir Humphrey D. B. Quinn (ed.), *The Voyages and Colonising Enterprises of Sir Humphrey Gilbert,* 2 vols (David Beers, London, 1940).

Gosson, Stephen *Plays Confuted in Five Actions* (1582; reprinted by Garland Publishing Inc., New York and London, 1973).

—— *The School of Abuse* (1579; reprinted by Garland Publishing Inc., New York and London, 1973).

Greene, Robert J. A. Lavin (ed.), *Friar Bacon and Friar Bungay* (?1589–90, Ernest Benn, London, 1969).

Harrison, G. B. (ed.) *The Elizabethan Journals; being a record of those things most talked of during the years 1591–1603* (Routledge, London, 1955).

Holinshed, Raphael et al *Holinshed's Chronicles of England, Scotland and Ireland,* 6 vols (1587; reprinted by AMS Press Inc., New York, 1965).

Jonson, Ben Douglas Brown (ed.), *The Alchemist* (1610, Ernest Benn, London, 1966).

Judges, A. V. (ed.) *The Elizabethan Underworld; A Collection of Tudor and early Stuart Tracts and Ballads telling of the Lives and Misdoings of Vagabonds, Thieves, Rogues and Cozeners* (Routledge & Kegan Paul, London, 1930).

Kempe, William *A Dutiful Invective against the most heinous Treasons of Ballard and Babington* (Richard Jones, London, 1587).

Kyd, Thomas J. R. Mulryne (ed.), *The Spanish Tragedy* (?1585–7, A. & C. Black, London, 1989).

Lemon, R. et al (eds) *Calendar of State Papers, Domestic Series,* volumes covering from 1547 to 1603 (Longman, London, 1856 and subsequently).

Luther, Martin *On War Against the Turk* (1529; reprinted in Jaroslav Pelikan and Helmut T. Lehmann (eds), *Luther's Works,* 55 vols, 46, Fortress Press, Philadelphia, 1967).

Machiavelli, Niccolò *The Art of War* (1595 edn; reprinted by Theatrum Orbis Terrarum Ltd, Amsterdam, 1969).

—— Bernard Crick (ed.), *The Discourses* (Penguin Books, Harmondsworth, 1961).

—— *The Florentine History* (1595 edn; reprinted by David Nutt, London, 1905).

—— George Bull (ed.), *The Prince* (Penguin Books, Harmondsworth, 1971).

Maclure, Millar (ed.) *Marlowe: The Critical Heritage 1588–1896* (Routledge & Kegan Paul, London, 1979).

Mulcaster, Richard (?) *The Quenes Majesties Passage through the City of London to Westminster the day before her Coronation* (1559; reprinted by Yale University Press, New Haven, 1960).

Nelson, Thomas *A Short Discourse: Expressing the Substance of all the late pretended Treasons against the Queenes Majestie, and Estates of this Realme, by sundry Traitors* (G. Robinson, London, 1587).

Penry, John et al *Marprelate Tracts* (1588–9; reprinted by Scholar Press, Leeds, 1967).

Rabelais, François J.M. Cohen (trans.), *Gargantua and Pantagruel* (Penguin Books, London, 1987).

Rainoldes, John et al *Th' Overthrow of Stage-Players* (1599;

reprinted by Garland Publishers Inc., New York and London, 1974).

Ralegh, Sir Walter *The History of the World* (Walter Burre, London, 1614).

Rich, Barnaby *A New Description of Ireland* (Thomas Adams, London, 1610).

Scot, Reginald *The Discoverie of Witchcraft* (1584; reprinted by Elliot Stock, London, 1886).

Shakespeare, William, Andrew S. Cairncross (ed.), *2 Henry VI* (?1590, Methuen & Co. Ltd, London, 1957).

—— Brian Gibbons (ed.), *Romeo and Juliet* (?1591–6, Methuen & Co. Ltd, London, 1980).

—— E. A. J. Honigmann (ed.), *King John* (? 1594, Methuen & Co. Ltd, London, 1959).

—— Kenneth Muir (ed.), *Macbeth* (1606, Methuen & Co. Ltd, London, 1962).

—— John Russell Brown (ed.), *The Merchant of Venice* (? 1595–8, Methuen & Co. Ltd, London, 1961).

—— Peter Ure (ed.), *Richard II* (1595, Methuen & Co. Ltd, London, 1961).

Sherley, Sir Antony *Relation of his Travels into Persia* (1613; reprinted by Gregg International, Farnborough, 1972).

Spencer, Edmund *A View of the Present State of Ireland* (1633; reprinted by Clarendon Press, Oxford, 1970 in an edition by W. L. Renwick).

Stow, John *The Survey of London* (1603; reprinted by J. M. Dent & Sons Ltd, London, 1912).

Stubbes, John *The Discoverie of a Gaping Gulf whereinto England is like to be swallowed by another French marriage* (1579; reprinted by University Press of Virginia, Charlottesville, 1968).

Stubbes, Philip *The Anatomy of Abuses* (1583; reprinted by Trubner, London, 1877–82 for the New Shakespeare Society).

Whetstone, George *The Censure of a Loyall Subject* (Richard Jones, London, 1587).

The Dramatised Society

Anglo, Sydney *Spectacle, Pageantry and Early Tudor Policy* (Clarendon Press, Oxford, 1969).

Anglo, Sydney (ed.) *The Damned Art: Essays in the Literature of Witchcraft* (Routledge & Kegan Paul, London, 1977).

Ariès, Philippe *The Hour of Our Death*, Helen Weaver (trans:) (Penguin Books, Harmondsworth, 1981).

Bahktin, Mikhail *Rabelais and his World*, H. Iswolsky (trans.) (MIT Press, Cambridge, Massachusetts, 1968).

Bakeless, John *The Tragicall History of Christopher Marlowe*, 2 vols (Archon Books, Hamden, Connecticut, 1964).

Beier, A. L. *Masterless Men: The Vagrancy Problem in England 1560–1640* (Methuen, London and New York, 1985).

Beier, A. L., and Finlay, Roger (eds) *London 1500–1700: The Making of the Metropolis* (Longman, London, 1986).

Bellamy, J. *The Tudor Law of Treason: An Introduction* (Routledge & Kegan Paul, London, 1979).

Bergeron, D. M. *English Civic Pageantry 1558–1642* (Arnold, London, 1971).

Brady, Ciaran 'Spencer's Irish Crisis: Humanism and Experience in the 1590s', *Past and Present*, 111, 1986, pp. 17–49.

Bray, Alan *Homosexuality in Renaissance England* (Gay Men's Press, London, 1982).

—— 'Homosexuality and the Signs of Male Friendship in Elizabethan England', *History Workshop*, 29, 1990, pp. 1–19.

Burke, Peter *Popular Culture in Early Modern Europe* (Wildwood House, Aldershot, 1988).

Canny, Nicholas P. *From Reformation to Restoration: Ireland 1534–1660* (Helican, Dublin, 1987).

Chew, Samuel C. *The Crescent and the Rose: Islam and England during the Renaissance* (Oxford University Press, New York, 1937).

Clark, Sandra *The Elizabethan Pamphleteers: Popular Moralistic Pamphlets 1580–1640* (Athlone Press, London, 1983).

Clark, Stuart 'Inversion, Misrule and Witchcraft', *Past and Present*, 87, 1980, pp. 98–127.

Cooper, William Durrant 'Notices of Anthony Babington of Dethick', *Reliquary*, April 1862.

Costello, William T. *The Scholastic Curriculum at Early*

Seventeenth-Century Cambridge (Harvard University Press, Cambridge, Massachusetts, 1958).

Davis, Natalie Zemon *Society and Culture in Early Modern France: Eight Essays* (Duckworth, London, 1975).

Deacon, Richard *A History of the British Secret Service* (Frederick Muller Limited, London, 1969).

de Kalb, Eugenie 'An Elucidation of the Death of Christopher Marlowe through an Examination into the Lives and Interests of Certain of his Associates', unpublished Cambridge Ph.D. thesis, 1928.

—— 'Robert Poley's movements as a Messenger of the Court, 1588 to 1601', *Review of English Studies*, 9, 1933, pp. 13–18.

Eccles, Mark *Christopher Marlowe in London* (Harvard University Press, Cambridge, Massachusetts, 1934).

Edgerton, Samuel Y. *Pictures and Punishment: Art and Criminal Punishment during the Florentine Renaissance* (Cornell University Press, Ithaca and London, 1985).

Fletcher, Anthony and Stevenson, John (eds) *Order and Disorder in Early Modern England* (Cambridge University Press, 1965).

Foucault, Michel *Discipline and Punish: The Birth of the Prison*, Alan Sheridan, (trans.), (Penguin Books, Harmondsworth, 1977).

Freeman, Arthur 'Marlowe, Kyd and the Dutch Church Libel', *English Literary Renaissance*, 3, 1973, pp. 44–52.

French, Peter *John Dee: The World of an Elizabethan Magus* (Ark Paperbacks, London, 1987).

Fussner, F. Smith *The Historical Revolution: English Historical Writing and Thought 1580–1640* (Columbia University Press, New York, 1962).

Greenblatt, Stephen *Sir Walter Ralegh: The Renaissance Man and His Roles* (Yale University Press, New Haven and London, 1973).

Gwyer, J. 'The Case of Dr Lopez, *Transactions of the Jewish Historical Society of England*, 16, 1952, pp. 163–84.

Henderson, Philip *Christopher Marlowe* (Harvester, Brighton, 1974).

Hoffman, Calvin *The Murder of the Man who was Shakespeare* (Max Parrish, London, 1955).

Hotson, Leslie *The Death of Christopher Marlowe* (Nonesuch Press, London, 1925).

Jardine, Lisa 'The Place of Dialectic Teaching in Sixteenth Century Cambridge', *Studies in the Renaissance*, 21, 1974, pp. 31–62.

—— 'Humanism in the Sixteenth Century Cambridge Arts Course', *History of Education*, 4, 1975, pp. 16–31.

Kantorowitz, E. H. *The King's Two Bodies: A Study of Medieval Political Theology* (Princeton University Press, 1957).

Lamont, William M. *Godly Rule: Politics and Religion 1603–60* (Macmillan, London, 1969).

Manning, R. B. *Village Revolts: Social Protest and Popular Disturbances in England 1509–1640* (Clarendon Press, Oxford, 1986).

Nicholls, David 'The Theatre of Martyrdom in the French Reformation', *Past and Present*, 121, 1988, pp. 49–73.

Nichols, J. *The Progresses and Public Processions of Queen Elizabeth*, 3 vols (John Nichols and Son, London, 1823).

Pendry, E. D. *Elizabethan Prisons and Prison Scenes*, 2 vols (Universität Salzburg, 1974).

Pitkin, Hanna Fenichel *Fortune is a Woman: Gender and Politics in the Thought of Niccolò Machiavelli* (University of California Press, Berkeley, 1984).

Rabb, Felix *The English Face of Machiavelli: A Changing Interpretation* (Routledge & Kegan Paul, London, 1964).

Read, Conyers *Mr Secretary Walsingham and the Policy of Queen Elizabeth*, 3 vols (Clarendon Press, Oxford, 1925).

Rebhorn, Wayne A. *Foxes and Lions: Machiavelli's Confidence Men* (Cornell University Press, Ithaca and London, 1988).

Rhodes, Neil *The Elizabethan Grotesque* (Routledge & Kegan Paul, London, 1980).

Screech, M. A. *Rabelais* (Duckworth, London, 1979).

Seaton, Ethel 'Robert Poley's Ciphers', *Review of English Studies*, 7, 1931, pp. 137–50.

Sharpe, J. A. *Crime in Seventeenth-Century England: A County Study* (Cambridge University Press, 1983).

—— *Crime in Early Modern England 1550–1750* (Longman, London, 1984).

—— 'Last Dying Speeches: Religion, Ideology and Public Execution in Seventeenth-Century England', *Past and Present*, 107, 1985, pp. 144–67.

Sinfield, Alan *Literature in Protestant England 1560–1660* (Croom Helm, London, 1983).

Skinner, Quentin *The Foundations of Modern Political Thought* , 2 vols (Cambridge University Press, 1978).

Slack, Paul *The Impact of Plague in Tudor and Stuart England* (Routledge & Kegan Paul, London, 1985).

Smith, Alan Gordon *The Babington Plot* (Macmillan, London, 1936).

Stallybrass, Peter and White, Allon *The Politics and Poetics of Transgression* (Methuen, London, 1986).

Stone, Lawrence *The Crisis of the Aristocracy 1558–1641* (Clarendon Press, Oxford, 1965).

Spierenburg, Pieter *The Spectacle of Suffering: Executions and the Evolution of Repression: From a Preindustrial Metropolis to the European Experience* (Cambridge University Press, 1984).

Thomas, Keith *Religion and the Decline of Magic: Studies in Popular Beliefs in Sixteenth and Seventeenth-Century England* (Penguin, Harmondsworth, 1973).

—— *Rule and Misrule in the Schools of Early Modern England* (University of Reading, 1976).

Underdown, David, *Revel, Riot and Rebellion: Popular Politics and Culture in England 1603–1660* (Clarendon Press, Oxford, 1985).

Urry, William *Christopher Marlowe and Canterbury* (Faber & Faber, London, 1988).

Walker, D. P. *The Decline of Hell: Seventeenth-Century Discussions of Eternal Torment* (Routledge & Kegan Paul, London, 1964).

Wernham, R. B. 'Christopher Marlowe at Flushing in 1592', *English Historical Review*, 91, 1976, pp. 344–5.

Wilson, F. P. *The Plague in Shakespeare's London* (Oxford University Press, 1963).

The Drama

∨ Aers, David (ed.) *Medieval Literature: Criticism, Ideology and History* (Harvester, Brighton, 1986).

✗ Armstrong, W. A. *Marlowe's Tamburlaine: The Image and the Stage* (University of Hull Press, 1966).

∨ Asibong, Emmanuel B. *Comic Sensibility in the Plays of Christopher Marlowe* (Arthur H. Stockwell Ltd., Ilfracombe, 1979).

Barber, C. L. *Shakespeare's Festive Comedy: A Study of Dramatic Form and its Relation to Social Custom* (Princeton University Press, 1959).

—— ** *Creating Elizabethan Tragedy: The Theater of Marlowe and Kyd* (Chicago University Press, Chicago and London, 1988).

Battenhouse, Roy W. *Marlowe's Tamburlaine: A Study in Renaissance Moral Philosophy* (Vanderbilt University Press, Nasheville, 1941).

Beckwith, Sarah 'The Power of Devils and the Hearts of Men: Notes towards a Drama of Witchcraft', forthcoming.

Bergeron, David M. (ed.) *Pageantry in the Shakespearean Theater*. (University of Georgia Press, Athens, 1985).

Bevington, David M. *From Mankind to Marlowe: Growth of Structure in the Popular Drama of Tudor England* (Harvard University Press, Cambridge, Massachusetts, 1962).

Birringer, J. H. *Marlowe's Dr Faustus and Tamburlaine: Theological and Theatrical Perspectives* (Peter Lang, Frankfurt, 1984).

Boas, F. S. *Christopher Marlowe: A Biographical and Critical Study* (Clarendon Press, Oxford, 1940).

Boyette, Purvis 'Wanton Humour and Wanton Poets: Homosexuality in Marlowe's *Edward II*', *Tulane Studies in English*, 12, 1977, pp. 33–50.

Briggs, Julia ** 'Marlowe's *Massacre at Paris:* A Reconsideration', *Review of English Studies*, 34, 1983, pp. 257–78.

Bristol, Michael D. *Carnival and Theatre: the Plebeian Culture and the Structure of Authority in Renaissance England* (Methuen, London, 1985).

Brockbank, Philip *Marlowe's Doctor Faustus* (Edward Arnold, London, 1962).

Brooke, Nicholas 'The Moral Tragedy of Doctor Faustus', *Cambridge Journal*, 5, 1952, pp. 662–87.

—— ** 'Marlowe the Dramatist' in John Russell Brown and Bernard Harris (eds), *Elizabethan Theatre* (Edward Arnold, London, 1966), pp. 87–105.

—— *Horrid Laughter in Jacobean Tragedy* (Open Books, London, 1979).

Burnett, Mark Thornton 'Tamburlaine: An Elizabethan Vagabond', *Studies in Philology*, 84, 1987, pp. 308–23.

Chambers, E. K. *The Elizabethan Stage,* 4 vols (Clarendon Press, Oxford, 1923).

Cole, Douglas ** *Suffering and Evil in the Plays of Christopher Marlowe* (Princeton University Press, 1962).

Craik, T. W. *The Tudor Interlude: Stage, Costume and Acting* (Leicester University Press, 1958).

Dessen, Alan C. *Elizabethan Drama and the Viewer's Eye* (University of North Carolina Press, Chapel Hill, 1977).

—— *Elizabethan Stage Conventions and Modern Interpreters* (Cambridge University Press, 1984).

Dollimore, Jonathan ** *Radical Tragedy: Religion, Ideology and Power in the Drama of Shakespeare and his Contemporaries* (Harvester, Brighton, 1984).

Dollimore, Jonathan and Sinfield, Alan (eds) ** *Political Shakespeare: New Essays in Cultural Materialism* (Manchester University Press, 1985).

Drakakis, John (ed.) *Alternative Shakespeares* (Methuen, London, 1985).

Eliot, T. S. 'Christopher Marlowe', *Selected Essays* (Faber & Faber, London, 1951), pp. 118–25.

Empsom, William *Faustus and the Censor: The English Faust-Book and Marlowe's Doctor Faustus* (Basil Blackwell, Oxford, 1987).

Fieler, Frank B. *Tamburlaine, Part 1, and its Audiences* (University of Florida Press, Gainesville, 1962).

Friedenreich, K. et al (eds) ** *A Poet and a Filthy Play-maker: New Essays on Marlowe* (AMS Press, New York, 1988).

Gatti, Hilary *The Renaissance Drama of Knowledge: Giordano Bruno in England* (Routledge, London and New York, 1989).

Geckle, George L. *Tamburlaine and Edward II: Text and Performance* (Macmillan Education, Basingstoke, 1988).

Gill, Roma ** 'Marlowe's Virgil: *Dido Queene of Carthage*', *Review of English Studies*, 28, 1977, pp. 141–55.

—— ** 'Such Conceits as Clownage keeps in pay: Comedy and Doctor Faustus', in P.V.A. Williams (ed.), *The Fool and the Trickster: Studies in Honour of Enid Welsford* (Brewer, Cambridge, 1979), pp. 55–63.

Goldberg, Jonathan 'Sodomy & Society: The Case of Christopher Marlowe', *Southwest Review*, 69, 1984, pp. 371–8.

Greenblatt, Stephen ** *Renaissance Self-fashioning from More to Shakespeare* (University of Chicago Press, Chicago and London, 1980).

—— *Shakespearean Negotiations: The Circulation of Social Energy in Renaissance England* (Clarendon Press, Oxford, 1988).

Greg, W. W. (ed.) *Marlowe's Doctor Faustus 1604–1616: Parallel Texts* (Clarendon Press, Oxford, 1950).

Gurr, Andrew ** *The Shakespearean Stage 1574–1642* (Cambridge University Press, 1970).

—— *Playgoing in Shakespeare's London* (Cambridge University Press, 1987).

Harris, Anthony *Night's Black Agents: Witchcraft and Magic in Seventeenth-Century English Drama* (Manchester University Press, 1980).

Hattaway, Michael ** *Elizabethan Popular Theatre: Plays in Performance* (Routledge & Kegan Paul, London, 1982).

Hunter, G. K. 'The Theology of Marlowe's *The Jew of Malta*', *Journal of the Warburg and Courtauld Institutes*, 17, 1964, pp. 211–40.

Jardine, Lisa *Still Harping on Daughters: Women and Drama in the Age of Shakespeare* (Harvester, Brighton, 1983).

Jones, Robert C. *Engagement with Knavery: Point of View in Richard III, The Jew of Malta, Volpone and The Revenger's Tragedy* (Duke University Press, Durham, 1986).

Kahn, Coppelia *Man's Estate: Masculine Identity in Shakespeare* (University of California Press, Berkeley, 1981).

Kelsall, Malcolm *Christopher Marlowe* (E. J. Brill, Leiden, 1981).

Kernan, Alvin (ed.) ** *Two Renaissance Mythmakers: Christopher Marlowe and Ben Jonson* (Johns Hopkins University Press, Baltimore and London, 1977).

Kocher, Paul *Christopher Marlowe: A Study of his Thought, Learning and Character* (University of North Carolina Press, Chapel Hill, 1946).

Kott, Jan *The Bottom Translation: Marlowe and Shakespeare and the Carnival Tradition*, Daniela Miedzyrzecka and Lillian Vallee (trans.), (Northwestern University Press, Evanston, 1987).

Kuriyama, Constance B. *Hammer or Anvil: Psychological Patterns in Christopher Marlowe's Plays* (Rutgers University Press, New Brunswick, 1980).

Leech, Clifford '*Edward II*: Power and Suffering', *Critical Quarterly*, 1, 1959, pp. 181–96.

——— ** *Christopher Marlowe: Poet for the Stage* (AMS Press, New York, 1986).

Leech, Clifford (ed.) *Marlowe: A Collection of Critical Essays* (Prentice-Hall, Inc., Englewood Cliffs, New Jersey, 1964).

Levin, Harry ** *The Overreacher: A Study of Christopher Marlowe* (Harvard University Press, Cambridge, Massachusetts, 1952).

Mangan, Michael *Doctor Faustus: A Critical Study* (Penguin Masterstudies, Harmondsworth, 1987).

Minshull, Catherine 'Marlowe's Sound Machevill', *Renaissance Drama*, 13, 1982, pp. 35–53.

Morris, Brian (ed.) *Christopher Marlowe* (Ernest Benn, London, 1968).

Mullaney, Steven ** *The Place of the Stage: License, Play and Power in Renaissance England* (University of Chicago Press, Chicago and London, 1988).

Omerod, David and Wortham, Christopher (eds) *Christopher Marlowe: Dr Faustus: The A-Text* (University of Western Australia Press, Nedlands, 1985).

Orgel, Stephen *The Illusion of Power: Political Theater in the English Renaissance* (University of California Press, Berkeley, 1975).

Ribner, Irving 'Marlowe and Machiavelli', *Comparative Literature*, 6, 1954, pp. 348–56.

Ricks, Christopher '*Doctor Faustus* and Hell on Earth', *Essays in Criticism*, 35, 1985, pp. 101–20.

Sales, Roger *Much Ado About Nothing: A Critical Study* (Penguin Masterstudies, Harmondsworth, 1987).

Sanders, Wilbur *The Dramatist and the Received Idea: Studies in the Plays of Marlowe and Shakespeare* (Cambridge University Press, 1968).

Shepherd, Simon ** *Marlowe and the Politics of Elizabethan Theatre* (Harvester, Brighton, 1986).

Steane, J. B. *Marlowe: A Critical Study* (Cambridge University Press, 1974).

Summers, Claude J. *Christopher Marlowe and the Politics of Power* (Universität Salzburg, 1974)).

174   *Selected Bibliography*

Tennerhouse, Leonard *Power on Display: The Politics of Sha- kespeare's Genres* (Methuen, New York and London, 1986).
Thomson, Peter *Shakespeare's Theatre* (Routledge & Kegan Paul, London 1983).
Tulane *Tulane Drama Review: Marlowe Issue*, 8, Summer 1964.
Tydeman, William *Doctor Faustus: Text and Performance* (Mac- millan Education, Basingstoke, 1984).
Tydeman, William and Thomas, Vivien ** *Christopher Marlowe: A Guide through the Critical Maze* (The Bristol Press, 1989).
Weil, Judith ** *Christopher Marlowe: Merlin's Prophet* (Cam- bridge University Press, 1977).
Wickham, Glynne *Early English Stages 1300 to 1600*, volume two, part one, 1576 to 1660 (Routledge & Kegan Paul, London, 1963).
—— *The Medieval Theatre* (Cambridge University Press, 1987).
Wiles, David *Shakespeare's Clown: Actor and Text in the Elizabe- than Playhouse* (Cambridge University Press, 1987).
Williams, Raymond *Drama in a Dramatised Society: An Inaugural Lecture* (Cambridge University Press, 1975).
Wraith, Eugene *The Herculean Hero in Marlowe, Chapman, Shakespeare and Dryden* (Chatto & Windus, London, 1962).
Yates, Frances *The Occult Philosophy in the Elizabethan Age* (Ark Paperbacks, London, 1983).

Index